West Los Scandelous

WEST LOS SCANDELOUS

by
THE LEGENDARY ALI SHABAZZ

Cutty Mack
Publishing
los angeles

Cutty Mack Publishing

© 2018 The Legendary Ali Shabazz

legendaryalishabazz.com

Cover design by Dan Master
Interior layout by Lily J. Noonan

West Los Scandelous—1st ed.
ISBN 978-0-9987871-8-3 (print), ISBN 978-0-9987871-9-0 (digital)

DEDICATED TO
THE WESTSIDE TRIBE

CHAPTER 10

SHANNON PARKED THE CAR in the cut up the block and we walked down to Dante's crib. We both leapt over the three concrete steps onto the porch. Shannon rang the doorbell. When Dante answered the door, the look in his eyes showed that he was waiting for some mean pussy, not her nigga with evil intentions in his. Dante was actually tired of dealing with Shannon over his coke-abusing freak. He left the door open for us to let ourselves in and Dante turned around nonchalantly and went back to what he was doing. Dante and Soncho were playing Nintendo and the last thing on their mind was Shannon's bitch problems. Shannon must have been disturbed by their carefree attitude and took it upon himself to start looking all through Dante's pad like he was the police or some shit. Shannon flipped the mattress over in the bedroom and started pulling drawers out of the dresser. Shannon yanked the closets open, "Where's that bitch!"

Dante realized what was going on and jumped up from his game.

"What the fuck is wrong with you, Shannon? Don't be roaming through my crib looking for some freak bitch. I respect your Gangsta but you are not about to punk me in my own house."

Dante and Shannon started walking hard towards each other like they were ready to squab' but I jumped in between them and put a halt to that shit. Dante didn't feel like fucking off his high by dealing with Shannon's insecurities and just shrugged off the incident. He sat his

1

ass back down to finish his Techmo Bowl game. Dante said, "Fuck it, let him look for that hoe 'cuz she ain't here; go ahead and make a bigger fool of yourself, Shannon."

Shannon took his advice and went back to the bedroom to look in the other closet. I followed him, not to stop him from looking for Passion but to stop him from looking like a clown in front of everybody.

"Shannon, you are way out of bounds. This broad got you robbed. You are tripping off of her fucking Dante, but you should be worried about her fucking with those fools from the Number Blocks— our enemies, remember? And she's fucking with those fools from Mansfield and PBG."

"How you know it wasn't Dante who helped her rob me? You didn't think about how fast this fool came up, did you?"

"I seriously doubt if your little funky forty grand got him to this level 'cuz my nigga is balling right now," I responded with truth. Shannon's paper wasn't as long as he thought it was.

"Well, if he didn't do it, he knows something from fucking with that bitch Passion. He's got to watch his own ass so you know he quizzed the bitch. That's why I'm pissed! I know he knows something and he hasn't pulled my coattail or told me to keep my eyes open or nothing. This is bigger than tripping over a bitch. I'm just using that as a decoy until I find out what the fuck is going on. A wise man can always play a fool but a fool could never play a wise man. This is about trust and loyalty and dedication to this gangster life. We're all we got. I love Dante but he ain't never going to put in no work. He's Westside Mack all day but never a Gangster; the G just ain't in him. I'm about to rattle this cat's cage. I'm going to poke this fool's eyeball out with this ice pick and I bet you he starts talking." Shannon had his mind made up and started making his way to the front room.

BOOM!

We heard the front door bust open.

"What that…"

Pop! Pop! Pop!

"Gangsta like fool! Lay your bitch ass down!"

The name of the set the intruders claimed was deafened by the gunfire. Shannon ran and hid in the closet and I dove under the bed. Two more shots blasted off and we heard the hard thud of a body hitting the floor. We didn't know if it was Dante or Soncho. The mysterious voice in the other room started barking orders.

"One of y'all get the money out of the safe in the bedroom…hey bitch! You watch the door…I got these fools covered but if one of them even looks at me funny I'm going to blast these pretty dressed muthafuckas' skulls into a million fragments."

The voice sounded familiar but I couldn't put a face on it. I knew it was a gangster but from what set? My heart was beating like the speed of a racehorse. When the bedroom door opened all I could see was some dark blue Nikes coming toward the bed. The shoes were kind of small for a big nigga so it had to be a short punk or Shannon's bitch. I briefly thought about Baby Feet from Atlanta but he didn't walk too stable and would have easily been identified. I still didn't rule him out though. I was hoping somebody would say something again so I could match a face with a voice.

"Check under the bed, yo!" That was not what I was trying to hear. I nervously watched the small blue Nikes walk past the bed and into the bathroom.

"Hmmmm?" The inquisitive noise they made from the bathroom sounded like they came across something real good. It was 300,000 in cash and five kilos of pure Bolivian Coco that Dante had stashed away for a rainy day.

"What the fuck is taking you so long in there?" The voice from the front room was sounding irritated. It was also sounding familiar again. I was wondering if it was those fools from Hard-knock Killers' but we had got into so many confrontations with them in our lives I knew they didn't have the heart to pull this off. I tried to think hard but my mind had me thinking about trying to stay alive. I had no reason to take my pistol to Dante's so all I had to protect myself was instinct. I felt a shadow creeping by the foot of the bed. I could smell the stench of the Nikes they were so close. The intruder got on their knees to look under the bed. I had never been that shook up in my life. I held my breath. My mind told me to mutilate the first thing I saw. I saw a gloved hand raise the bedspread up.

"Fuck you! I got to get the homie to the hospital, get what you came for and get the fuck out!"

"What fool? You talking shit without a strap, Tubby? Shut ya fucking mouth, fat punk!" *Whop!*

Another thud came crashing down to the floor. Soncho getting cracked across is skull startled the intruder and I saw those Nikes scurry up to the front room. I was so tensed up I could feel my skin color turning back to normal after I exhaled.

"Shut the fuck up before I put two into your chubby boy ass! That nigga's going to be all right—I barely shot his ass!" The punk's arrogant voice was sounding so familiar it was driving me crazy.

"Should we just kill these niggas or what?" I heard some mumbles and grumbling I didn't hear before. Now I was starting to believe it was more than just two of them. The Ring Leader spoke,

"Hey fat boy, you wanna live? Fly this kite. Tell your boy Shannon he was lucky he wasn't at the crib when we robbed his bitch ass. I couldn't wait to murder that muthafucka, I wanted his life more than the money because it's personal!"

I could feel Shannon in the closet biting a hole in his bottom lip. I was really hoping Shannon didn't jump out the closet with that oriental fist knife thinking he was going to do some damage against that fire power. Shannon was sick like that but he maintained. Two bodies entered in the room. I heard one of them taking Dante's jewelry out of the drawers and I guess the other one was packing up the goodies they found in the bathroom.

The voice from the living room yelled out, "Let's get up out of here, cuz, and don't forget to hit that closet. This bitch ass nigga got some dope ass guns in there."

I no longer feared for Shannon's life when I heard that. I was just hoping Shannon had control over his emotions.

"Hurry up , you silly bitch!" The voice was so recognizable it was giving me a damn headache. Every step the intruder made toward the closet my heart beat faster.

I vaguely heard the voice in the front say *"...and I put that on Crip."* BAM! It hit me. I knew who was behind the sound of the voice. I was sure Shannon figured it by now, too. A masked intruder yanked the closet door open Shannon was hiding in and was immediately blinded by darkness seconds before he lost his life. Shannon threw a winter coat over the intruder's head and grabbed him around the mouth to drown the sound as he drove his knife through the mark's Adam's apple until it came out of the back of his neck. Shannon laid him down easy as he bent his knee to the floor. Shannon quickly slid two 9mm's under the bed. I started feeling very confident that we would make it out there by any means necessary.

Soon as I made it to my feet, one of them little niggas walked hard into the back room and made direct eye contact with Shannon. He didn't see me standing off to the side or what was coming next. Put one gun in that nigga's ear and the other one to the side of his dome and let them thangs go! I blew that muthafucka's head straight through that cheap plastered wall. Shannon stepped over the bodies and started making his way to the front room. I was right by his side, pistols still smoking.

"Ohhhh, here comes the surfer boys! If you think I'm gonna let some Westside niggas in OP shorts punk me, you got me fucked up!" said Crip Crazy as he stood his ground with his pistol pointed directly at Shannon. Passion was standing over Soncho with a revolver but now she had it pointed at me. That bitch was high on that shit plus she already saw that good pure Bolivian coke Dante had stashed. Passion became the most dangerous muthafucka in the room. Her loyalty lies with that Coco, She fucked 3 of the niggas in this room and not one of em's dick was better than that Bolivian cocaine. Shannon was hurting but he never made eye contact with Passion. He was preoccupied with a hateful individual that had no other desires in life but to kill him.

"You all right, Soncho?" Shannon asked to break the tension and see where Crip Crazy's head was. The bump on Soncho's head was the least of his concerns.

"Yeah, I'm cool. Just a lil dizzy from the butt of that pistol."

"Come on over here next to us. You all right, Dante?"

"Hell naw nigga! I'm shot!" Dante spoke Truth sounding like he was he was stricken with pain.

Shannon tossed Soncho two more guns as he got to his feet.

Now here we were face-to-face in a hood standoff. Guns pointed. Fingers on triggers. No arms are getting tired. Nobody is looking nervous, but everybody is looking for one weakness to exploit, just one little excuse to justify the next move.

This little punk nigga had six pistols pointed directly at his ass. Passion was strapped, but she was not the down bitch he needed in his corner right now. Crip Crazy sensed her weakness so he snatched Passion by her hair and put her skinny neck in a tight headlock and used her as a shield as he said, "Drop those guns before I kill this bitch!"

We all looked at each with our eyebrows frowned like *this nigga must be crazy.* Just for saying some shit like that we lit that Bitch up! We left Crip Crazy standing looking spooked and shit.

"That was *his* bitch, not mine!" I stated to no one in particular and started packing up everything important and non-incriminating in Dante's crib. I didn't look at Shannon. I didn't want to know if he was hurt because we popped that silly bitch that he happened to be in love with. I quite sure he felt some way about it. He had that stinging sensation in his nose like he was on the verge to shedding a tear but that beast in him was ready to channel that aggression and mixed feelings on one nigga. I knew Shannon wanted to end his personal beef with Crip Crazy on a bad note so I let him handle it. Shannon didn't waste his time giving a movie scene speech before he killed homie. He just started letting loose. I knew homie was dead after the second shot but Shannon just kept shootin'.

As I packed the bags, Soncho helped Dante to his feet and Shannon was still shootin' that punk muthafucka until nothing was left in both clips. We cleaned out the crib the best we could and left to get the homie Dante some medical attention.

On the way out the door Soncho looked down and thought about shooting the dead man. 32 holes didn't leave much for him so he let it go.

"Damn Shannon. You're an extremist in everything you do. Why you have to shoot that muthafucka 32 times?

"Cuz that was all I had in the clips!"

Chapter 11

NEW REGIME, NEW ROUTINE. That new day, same old shit slogan doesn't sit right with me. I'm not the same nigga I was yesterday. I blew a man's brain matter out his head and left it inside the plastered walls like asbestos. No incriminating evidence, no witnesses, and no murder weapons. The Crib was leased to a smoker that was already dead so the police just threw that case in the dead nigger files. I would have been leery of Shannon opening the case back up since he liked to share confidential information with other unsavory individuals so they would know he was not the one to be tested.

That kill was different. Shannon and the rest of us developed a serious aggressive look in our eyes. From that day forward, a level of maturity as well as the wolf-like instincts, the tenacity, commitment, and the will it took to be in this game just came over us. Shannon, Dante, Soncho, and myself as well as Dez, Khan, and Suge never spoke on the bodies we sent back to Beelzebub, not even amongst ourselves. It just happened like that. It wasn't our rule or a team philosophy; it was just meant to be.

That new look in our eyes offset by our beastly demeanor wasn't hard to detect either. Fools from the other side could see us coming now. Our skateboard clothes no longer disguised us. Now we stood out. *"That's those niggas from the Westside"* should have been a #1 record cuz that's all we heard every time we showed up on a set.

The Westside Gangster Macks did establish some unwritten rules, codes, and ethics once we realized we were serious about this game here. All that heinous bullshit Shannon use to do with Dirt Alley to the silly shit like shooting BB Guns for fun was gone. Drive-by shootings, gunplay over hood rat bitches or cuz we didn't like some goofy nigga that was out of pocket on that particular day was so far from the level we were taking this life to that after a while those adolescent baby-gangster games didn't even cross our field of play. We targeted an enemy and eliminated it up close and personal. We never put ourselves in a position where a civilian would have to view us handle business much less get caught in the crossfire unless it was a *the whole family must go* situation, then that would be our only exception to the rule.

Gangbanging over colors? The way we dress? That's not happenin'. Bloods and Crips are street gangs. They do what they do. We have some Blood homies and Crip partners that are good friends of ours and we do business with but I'm not qualified to speak on their culture. That's not us. The good friends from those gangs shared personal stories with me on several occasions on why they joined their particular set and there were many interests we did not share. Some of those brothers had horrific childhoods, abandonment, never been hugged or kissed by their Mom, no lights or heat in house, some parents plagued by drugs, child abuse, tire iron beatings, no food in the house for 3 days, and being on their own since they were 8 years old and shit, and the only place to find love, food, clothing, and shelter was from the neighborhood gang.

We never experienced any shit like that. Our parents may smoke a little weed and drink a little wine on the weekends and talk a lot of shit but that was about it. I couldn't imagine growing up with any food in the house for weeks in LA in the 80s. That was crazy. We had to be in the house when the streetlights came on to eat dinner. We complained cuz we didn't feel like eating that night cuz we wanted to play. My mama loved me, Shannon's mama tells me she loves me, all my homies' parents share love for us like we were their own. That's what makes us so fucked up. That's what makes us so dangerous. We didn't grow up in that life but we are about that life like it chose us.

So it had nothing to do with our upbringing, straying from the path our parents put us on, or our environment. I thought it could be genetics; everybody has a great-great grandfather that was a moonshine bootlegger or numbers runner but I doubt that gene skipped three generations and hit us at the same time so I threw that theory out. The only way to justify it is to say it was meant to be. I didn't want to fight it but I always paid attention to it.

There had to be a reason we were chosen for this life from out of our environment. We didn't know what the purpose was so everything we did we just planned to be the best at it until we figured that shit out. The "This life leads you to jail or the grave" cliché' would be tested not because of young arrogance but because of faith in our goals and the confidence of achieving them. We realized there was a bigger picture. We just couldn't see it clearly quite yet.

The biggest misconception about us since we didn't fit the criteria of what a gangster is supposed to be in our advisory's limited vision is that we weren't real. So since we didn't look a certain way or rolled a certain way we weren't doing real shit. What is real? Mail fraud is real, the con game is real, but a killer that wears khakis with a flag in the back pocket qualifies them as real. That philosophy always put us ten light years ahead of those shallow-thinking Negroes.

I admit we did look like the dudes that should be tested. If I fit the criteria of what a "Real Gangster" is supposed to look like I would look at us and say, "Oh, let's rob these Van-wearing niggas. They can't be serious. I know they're not shooters!" I could see their point of view, but I never agreed. The ones that thought like that are no longer here. They were real killers doing that real shit. Thinking about it now, they are right. We are not real niggas. I don't want to be that. It's too many real niggas dead or in jail from doing that real shit so no that's not what we want to do. But what we do want is to learn from these real niggas' mistakes. Knowledge is key in everything one does. My vision is bigger than a street corner. I love this gangster shit and I'm all in. You might not find us throwing up our set, but you best believe we're puttin' in work.

Now let me make this clear before I have you thinking we were some young bad super niggas that couldn't be touched. That was far from the case. I'm speaking specifically on the *criteria gangsters* that were jealous of us or thought we were soft because of our choice of clothing. We stayed smashing on them because they were coming at us as haters not gangsters. They weren't in it for the money. Now the wolves that prey on dealers and rob for a living I have the ultimate respect for them. Any man that can rob another man that is known for having a gun in is hand is a special breed. Anything can pop off at anytime. Sometimes it comes down to who was smarter a split second before the other. *Got em'* can go either way. I respect them because their intention is to get that money or product they came for first and foremost. Gunplay is secondary but a close second.

It's funny—not at the time it's happening, but looking back, some of those skilled professional jackers are some very mannerable and polite muthafuckas when they rob you. They tell you everything is going to be all right while they tying you up and taking all your gotdamn money. Some of them are assholes. They laugh and tell you *"I gotcha! I caught cha slippin'! Come up off that! And it ain't gon' be no problems!!"* And the one that just kills the mood is when a fool you never met before or will never see again that's been scoping you out, runs up on you real slick like with a gun to the rib cage and says, *"You already know what this is."* I salute those clever wolves, and over the years I've learned to work with them rather than against them.

Contrary to what the naysayers spew the *Real*-Real Gangsters loved us. We played our position. We did great business with them. We were respectful to our elders in the game, and they dug our style. The problem with my generation is we think we know everything by the time we are 16 because we did a little dirt in the streets. We always want to dismiss the old timers as *played out*. We want to boast that it's a new era. A true OG has no problem with a youngster that's serious about getting their money. They encourage it. It is cool with them that we have new rules as long as you respect the old ones. That's building and elevating.

Unfortunately, that's rare nowadays, especially in LA. There are more old cats that try to take advantage of us with trick knowledge rather than school us with street wisdom. It doesn't take long to figure them out. The sincere ones offer advice when you ask for it. The frauds are always telling us what we should be doing and it only benefits them. That's where conflict occurs because now it becomes a question of character and principle. We don't like the feeling of being used. In those cases an elder that should be respected turns into a regular old nigga that got to be dealt with just that quick.

With the majority of gangsters I've been around, the favorite topic to debate is *if they would rather be respected or feared.* It's referenced in all the gangster movies. The answer is always 50/50 either way. I eliminate those factors and look at a Gangster's character and his principles to determine if they should be respected or if it's somebody I don't want to cross in this game. I never look down on OGs that was on top of the world in a Penthouse Suite in the 70s and now they are lying in the gutter with a heroin needle in their arm. I study their story the most. Some had it coming and got there due to bad karma and some got there because of tragic personal circumstance so I was in no position to laugh at and judge who fell off or a has been and who was doing bad. I do judge the person that is constantly talking down on a person that fell off and obviously hasn't figured out how to get back up yet. Kicking a person while their down is punk shit to me. Then when the fallen victim gets up stronger than before that same punk is the one saying, *"He shouldn't be President of a company. I remember when he was a drug addict sleeping on he streets!"* I keep my eyes on the one that's always badmouthing. They don't want to see anybody else doing well.

I am committed to this life I chose. I have to accept everything that comes with it. Most importantly, I have to utilize this game to its full potential. I want more out of the underworld than most. I don't need to be on top of the world if I'm the only one up there. All the bitches, yeah, I want all the bitches that come with the game, but not at an expense.

But all jokes aside I don't want sugar. I need substance. I'm focused. I'm determined. *Lord, bless the ones that show me how to do wrong the right way, and for the souls I have to send back to you, let those be justified. I'm not asking for forgiveness of sins I willfully commit but please help me make sense of them and Have Mercy! Amen!*

$ $ $ $ $

IT'S OK TO HAVE NEW RULES BUT RESPECT THE OLD ONES!!

"What up, Shannon, how was your trip? You're back in town kind of quick," I asked when he rolled up on us at Meaty Meat Burgers.

"Maaaan, you know how I do it. I roll down to Kansas City and set up a little bullshit weed spot to feel everything out. I get in pretty good with the locals so now I'm ready to bring in the White shit. Right before I lace them with that white, I run into the homie Demetrio from Rolling 30's out there doing his thing. He said he got it poppin' in St. Louis and I can cut the quality shit I had to nothing and quadruple my money. I say fuck it and roll down there with this fool. It was poppin' like Demetrio said but he wasn't the one that had it like that. He needed that good shit to officially carry that title. Anyway, we run up on a couple of trustworthy individuals and put a business plan together. Now you know every town has their own slang right? Certain words mean different things to other people in different places."

"Oh shit, I already see where this story is going. I've been in that position before," Dez laughed and remembered the time he was in the county jail and broke this white boy's jaw that thought he was gay when he said he couldn't wait to get home and get some *Hot Cock*. The white boy moved away from Dez and said, "Hey dude. I didn't know you did dick—nothing personal but I can't be white and seen talking to somebody from the gay module. I have enough problems on my own." *Cock* means pussy in the hood; it means *penis* in the white culture. Simple mistake but it was a very costly one at the wrong place and time.

"You know what time it is, Dez. You see where this is going. Just the way we call each other Homie, they call each other *Durty.*"

"Ahhhhh naw, that's ugly…. and Demetrio is not the type of nigga that understands a difference in Culture. He can't stand when you call the 30's *Dirtys*… How did that turn out?"

"Even though it has nothing to do with our code, do I really need to dramatize that bullshit? And Demetrio was off that drank with a pistol in his hand. No need to explain that. I know he fucked off a lot of money over some fuckin' dialect. He laid that fool down—a good dude, too. Those cats don't play that shit. We were up outta there. I had Demetrio drop me off at the Greyhound. I didn't even want to ride with that fool," Shannon continued his story shaking his head.

I added in my two cents. "See, trying to work this game with these small level cats around us is not a good thing. They have no mental discipline, just all-aggressive emotion."

"These little fools don't know nothing about class, they shit be raggedy as hell and so violent. A fly touch can smooth a lot of shit out and keep everything sweet," Suge stated just like the cute little nigga he was, and of course, Dante agreed. They were peas of the same pod.

"Please speak on it, Playboy. I got in this game to mack money and honey—not beefs with these dummies."

"Who ordered me this plain hamburger with nothing on it? Y'all some scandalous individuals! This muthafucka looks dry as hell," Soncho was complaining about the dirty trick we pulled on him. I looked at all my soldiers in their eyes. This was the Westside. The nucleus of the crew. Everybody had a position and played it well. I had the vision and Shannon had the will to make it possible. Dez had the muscle; Khan had the knack to hustle. Dante and Suge kept things calm and orderly with the intent that everything we did would go smoothly, and Soncho kept our sanity with his happy personality. We all have different characters and hustles but there is one thing we all share in common that only comes into play when someone crosses us.

"I'm heading to the gym to get that work, y'all rollin'?" Dez asked as stretched his neck and rolled his shoulders as if they were getting tight.

"I'm down to roll with you, but I'm not holding those mitts while you box and I can't get my workout in." Dez nodded at me. So I accepted the offer under my conditions.

"I'm doing heavy bag work today. That's what Soncho is for," Dez replied as he threw a light playful left hook into Soncho's ribs that still hurt.

We all rolled to the grimy Main Street Gym in downtown Los Angeles right on the edge of Skid Row. Dante and Suge declined. Dante was still a couple of weeks behind the date the doctor said he can resume physical exercise. Suge was one of those Family Fitness membership ass niggas. He dressed nice when he worked out. Suge didn't want no parts of the stink, filth, and wretchedness of the Main Street Gym and Skid Row environment. We liked to go because of the symbolism of it. Great Champions in the World of Boxing have all been there one time or another. Hungry cats with aggressive attitudes are in that gym training hard, spittin' blood on the floor, and pushing themselves to their limits in order to achieve their goals and dreams. Just being around that type of energy does something to us. We walked in, sizing cats up and wondering how we would measure up to each of the men that returned our mad dog stares with the same thoughts in mind. Dez split from us and went into his boxing regimen. Soncho followed behind him. Khan, Shannon and I warmed up with a little jump rope and basic calisthenics.

"School will be starting again soon. Ain't you glad we don't have to put up with that shit this year?" I was talking to Shannon but I guess the subject matter was a little sensitive for Khan because he still had another year to go and the way his grades looked he might have another five to go.

"Speak for yourself when I'm not around. I still have to deal with that shit," Khan complained.

"That's crazy. You make more money than the teachers and the principal. You're going to spend half the year ditching anyway. Why don't you just get a GED or drop out?"

"Moms be trippin'. She's from the old school where a High School Diploma means something. It's a family tradition. Even if I made all A's, it wouldn't mean shit to me. I hate school that much. Shannon got his diploma on the wall, and that's enough for one house if you ask me," Khan retorted with his face frowned up like he was angry and sick.

"Don't encourage my brother to drop out of school. He needs to be in school to learn how to count, add, and subtract. He's always short with my money, careless with it, and always losing it somewhere. If he weren't my brother, I would have did something bad to him by now."

"You still tripping over the little $1,500 I lost at Magic Mountain? It fell out my pocket on the roller coaster. You gave it to me to hold. Don't put that shit on me."

"See what I'm saying… let him go to school. I know between the hours of 8am and 3pm, I'll have some peace," Shannon replied as he walked over to the speed bag and began his routine. Khan worked on the speed bag next to Shannon. The sibling rivalry continued as they competed on whom was the fastest hitting the Speed Bag versus who had the most power and quickness.

As we moved over to the weight benches, I quieted the brothers down with some tender conversation.

"Are we rolling with out with our ladies tonight or are we going to fuck around with some new bitches?" I had to put it out there like that so we could start getting mentally prepared. Those were two totally different worlds. Putting fire to our testosterone in the gym could take us either way. If we were going to drink and in one of those moods to get in some young dumb shit we were going to take broads that got excited around that type of hood activity.

"It depends… what's poppin' tonight?" Shannon asked. We were on the same page. It was a Saturday Night and anything was possible.

"Nothing really. No parties are jumping off so that means Westwood should be poppin' tonight."

"I overheard some cutie pies at the Pavilion saying they were rolling to Westwood. I'm down. I want to follow up on one I was checking out."

"Oh hell no! You know how Shannon gets down. He will have the cute one and her friends all look like Soncho… and not his body type. In the face!" Khan barked and it wasn't in a joking matter. Shannon is scandalous like that and Khan knows his brother well.

"Yeah, let's take our ladies out and make it a Civilian Night in Westwood. What's playing good at the movies?"

"We saw everything good already. We can go and see *Weird Science*, uh, Homeboy Pee Wee Herman from that Cheech and Chong flick got a solo movie out, and *Back to the Future,*" Khan read off a list of the things he really wanted to see. We didn't care. We were going to be tongue kissing and finger fuckin' half of the movie anyway. So we agreed on *Weird Science* 'cause we thought the song by the same name was cool.

I glanced over at Dez hitting the heavy bag. Damn, my nigga hits hard. Dez is a lean dude but his hands are nice. I was a fan. I hate when we get in club brawls 'cause I can't see Dez throw those things. I like a street side seat to see him thump with cats. Dez loved to fight, too. But unlike most Old School Dudes that pride themselves on solving differences with fist instead of guns, Dez could go either way depending on the day. He didn't prefer one method of violence to the other. He's shot muthafuckas he could have easily knocked out on a bad night on a couple of occasions. Dez is not a bully or evil individual per say but that muthafucka is dangerous with a quick sick temper. Dez was throwing hard vicious hooks into the heavy bag. He was leaving permanent dents in the spots he hit. Soncho was holding the bag and his thick body jerked every time Dez hit it with evil intentions. The young boxers as well as some of the older professionals that were gazing at his power could probably out box him, all lacked and wished they had that look in their eyes that Dez possessed. Dez had half the gym defeated without landing one punch. Dez was my ace boom but I know something wasn't all the way right with my dude. I didn't fear him but I'm glad he was on my side. We had a couple of schoolyard fights before as young locs. They were always broke up before a winner was determined. Shannon and Dez were another case. They fought twice with each one getting a victory. They often speak on breaking the tie eventually but as we get older, it's harder to find things that make you want to fight your best friend that you're putting serious big man work in with.

Dez walked over to the old legendary trainers like he always does after his routine to be graded on his skills. Besides his natural aggression and tenacity to want to beat men merciless, Dez learned where and how to hit a foe correctly from men that did it for a living. He knew that sweet science. Against another boxer with gloves on, the end results may end differently but in a street fight with the average gangbanger, they didn't have the skills to compete with Dez. That was the edge he was looking for. Dez had no desire to box for sport. Dez wanted to hand out beatdowns. The old trainers see the potential in Dez's punches but they never once pulled him to the side and gave him that pep talk like you see old dudes do in the Rocky movies. They never told him to channel his aggressions into boxing. They also saw the eyes of a young killer so they didn't really fuck with Dez personally. He was too unpredictable. A friendly sparring session could lead to something that has nothing to do with boxing. We often wondered why Dez was such a short fuse. He wasn't abused by his parents or attacked as a child but he's seen something along his journey that made him that way.

$ $ $ $ $

Westwood Village was the main shopping center in the Westwood district in the City of LA about a mile and some change from UCLA College. There were a lot of cute stores, shops, and restaurants owned by independent merchants along the blocks. They had 3 or 4 movie theaters and a couple of corporate chain stores looking for ways to overpower the small business owners. The City of Westwood is All-White; the word predominately doesn't even need to be used in front of it. Students at the school added a little color but take them away and one would think it was snowing in LA.

The migration of Blacks coming to Westwood in packs started with the popularity of Pac Man and pop lockin'. The Westwood Arcade was where it all went down. The scene was arcade games and breakdancing. As we got a little older, the scene started to evolve. Street performers, bigger crowds, bicycle cab rides, pretty girls and fly guys started to hang out in Westwood more frequently. Even with the migration of Black people, it was still a Westside thang. The kids were from Beverly Hills High and Palisades. The Blacks dressed Preppie in a lot of Ralph Lauren and Camp Beverly Hills clothing. The wannabe Prepsters were tricked into wearing outdated Flip Shirts, Shorts and Sperry Topsiders. The older Brothers that liked white chicks and to race mix went to Club Dillon's. So all those little elements involved that made Westwood the spot to be was just a precursor for grand daddy of them all, the UCLA Mardi Gras. The UCLA Mardi Gras is when Westwood was in rare form… for Black people and stylish whites alike. The Mardi Gras had been around for 50 years but in the 80s it got some serious soul. When we came on the scene, it took it to a whole 'nother level. It was still nice, friendly, and white during the daytime hours… When night hit, the Freaks came out!! It was basically a Carnival with a few rides, but we had fun just congregating.

$ $ $ $

We all came to Westwood together that night but we rode in separate cars. It was ladies night. It was about showing them a good time. Our plan was to watch a movie, get a bite to eat at Hamburger Hamlet, fall into Club Dillon's for a few drinks even though we were underage, and then be out for some personal intimacy. Well, at 18 it's more like rough fuckin'. It wasn't a strange vibe in the air that night but we did take notice when a pack of young thugs from Rolling O's Crip banged on us and threw up their set as they drove passed. Under civilized circumstances, OGs tend to give passes to rival gangsters on Family Day or Wifey Night if it's nothing serious between y'all personally. Young niggas don't give a fuck. They didn't even know we banged; they just hit us up just because they felt like it. We do that shit, too, when we're full off that liquor so we didn't point fingers. We just raised our antennas. Rolling O's never come out here to Westwood. Matter of fact no gangs east of LaBrea ever came to Westwood. We didn't know what that was all about. It was supposed to be a strapless night with our ladies but now we were looking at each other unsure if we should roll naked or not. Toni, Shari, London, April, Lu-Lu, and Janna had an idea of what we were about—you know, they heard things about us—but they never asked questions. They knew we owned guns, but they didn't know we carried them with us all the time. I left my strap in the car. Shannon and Dez treat a gun like an American Express

Card; they never leave home without it. Dez was just that type of nigga. Shannon had enemies he didn't know about. It was always a young thug looking to earn his stripes by killing Shannon. The biggest mistakes they make is they miss or fold up under the pressure. All Shannon needs is a split second to get him out of a dangerous situation and put his foe in a deadly one. Shannon already used up his 9 lives so he was past the point in giving a fuck. But I know it messed with his mind. It had to have.

We all held hands with our ladies as we walked slowly around the blocks waiting for the movie to start. The streets were packed as usual but we were in our own little world. We tried not to pay attention to what everybody else was doing just in case we were missing out on some single man fun. It was always some fine ass bitches in Westwood to fuck with. We window-shopped a lot to keep our "*heads*" out of the street.

Shannon saw this sweet Ralph Lauren sweater he had to buy. We could tell his lady Janna wanted something nice, too, but Shannon is tight with his money like that. He didn't buy her shit. We don't trick. All that *"I need to get my hair and nails done"* shit was for them South Central and Eastside muthafuckas. We are about having a great time. Whatever we have, our ladies have, but we don't do cash handouts. We weren't about to take penitentiary chances and then give our money to some untrustworthy bitch for some pussy. We were getting pussy when we were broke so why pay for it now? These were our main ladies but none of us was planning on getting married to them. They earned a different level of respect from us so we treated them a little differently.

The movie was a'ight but the hand and head job I got in the back row of the theater was worthy of the Academy Award. Shannon should have gone to the Pussy Cat Theater. He was fuckin' Janna. Shannon says she gives terrible head. She's all teeth and no skill so he did what he usually does and took it to the extreme. They had the whole theater smelling like pussy and popcorn.

When we left the theater, it was active outside. We saw and mingled with all our friends we went to high school with. It was a nice mix of races out on the streets socializing and strolling up the blocks. After slapping fives and giving bro' hugs, we went into Hamburger Hamlet to get our grub on.

I was checking out our ladies. They were good girls but they were attracted to that life. I wasn't sure if they could hold up under the pressure if shit got thick because they had never been tested. I was really starting to dig my woman Toni and the feeling was mutual. We complemented each other. But it was best if I schooled her early if she planned to go along on this interesting ride. We excused ourselves from the group and sat at a private table off in the corner of the restaurant.

"Oh, look at the little love birds flying to their separate nest. Ashamed to hang with their loud-ass friends," Khan teased us.

We both flipped him the middle finger. "Here's your Love Bird muthafucka, two of 'em! Now watch us spread our wings." We flipped him another bird with our free hand and held them up. We gave him a wink. Toni locked her arm around mine and we strolled to our seat.

"Toni, I want to talk to you about something serious. I'm really starting to dig you in a real way. How do you feel about the time you spent with me so far over the past few months?"

"To be honest Trav, I wasn't trying to push the issue and make you feel locked down at 18 years old so I didn't say anything but now that you asked, I've been in love with you since the day we met. You have a mystique and leadership quality about yourself that is so sexy to me. The way you talk with your hands and—don't laugh—but even the way you grab your dick in certain conversations just *whooooooo!* Makes me want to listen and cream my panties when you speak and all eyes are on you. Now don't take what I'm saying as I'm looking at you for sex. I'm talking about the manly sex appeal that comes from your strength: the strength you exude, the respect you give and get in return, and that is a rare quality. You're an avid reader, you play chess in the park, and you make intelligent decisions. That is what I'm attracted to and those other things, too. You have a brain in *both heads*," Toni laughed as she concluded her feelings about me.

"That's cool, baby. I dig that but it can also pose a problem. What I do for a living takes a down and dirty broad if you feel what I'm saying. I'm not expecting you to do know hood rat shit like traveling with dope or killin' some nigga in a drive-by but lying on the witness stand to keep my Black Ass out of jail, educating yourself and helping me do the right thing with my money and not dreaming of spending it on some bullshit. A down ass woman that can play the part of a down and dirty broad. I hope that gave you a clearer picture of what I meant by that title," I expounded on my statement. I looked at Toni directly in her eyes and she didn't flinch a muscle in her face. She had no girly smile, no *I don't know about this* frown, no emotions, and no warning signs in her eyes that read caution. Now she had me wondering.

"I know what you're about, Trav. I'm familiar with certain aspects of the life. My father is a confidence artist. He worked a lot on the east coast but schooled in the midwest... I believe that's the story or in the reverse order. You know that con game is tricky so he might tell us he's in one place and be somewhere totally different. Right now he's in Terminal Island. He'll be home soon. My dad uses his wits but I know if there is a bag of 50k or more and the true owner of it says *you are going to have to shoot me for it*, Pops will shoot them before the sentence is finished."

"I like my father-in-law already. But how is he going to feel about his baby girl getting involved with a man like me?"

"I'm Daddy's baby girl, of course he's not going to like it but he will accept it if I'm serious about you. He definitely ain't going to give me that old bullshit speech, *You can be with anybody, baby girl, like a doctor or a lawyer.* He knows half the doctors are freaks and licensed drug dealers and he would never want me to be with a shiesty ass lawyer that locks good niggas up. Once he see's how serious I am about you, he's going to sit me down and school me about what it takes to be a woman in that life and the instructions I must follow to hold you down. He's a real one.

And I am, too, Trav. My home girls over there—a couple of them are sincere and a couple of them are just happy good girls that like bad guys. Lu Lu and Shari, I cant really gauge how they would respond under pressure but I would be nervous if they were being interrogated alone in a room so you might want to pull Soncho and Dez coattail to that. I love you, Trav. I just hope I didn't show my hand too soon. Like I said we're young. Women are emotional. I've already thought about our life together. I'm not here to run you off. I'm here to be by your side," said Toni as she spilled out her feelings. She opened her purse and showed me my 9mm Beretta and closed it. "That was not to show you I'm down to pack a gat for you. I'm not that. I know we are out here with Shannon and Dez's crazy asses and they are strapped with the safety off. Anything can jump off with those two, and I'd rather you have yours to protect both of us than get caught without it thinking you are protecting me from the life. I got you, Trav."

She sure did. From that moment forward our relationship got real serious.

As we exited Hamburger Hamlet, we were hit up in a friendly way by some rolling fools in a Chevy Lumina. We found that interesting. They don't come to this side of town either. Shannon and Khan threw our set up. Dez kept his hands in his peacoat. Suge and Soncho gave them the head nod. I moved one eyebrow but in the dark along with my complexion I doubt if it was seen. We had no beefs with crews outside our jurisdiction, I don't think, so we continued going about our way. As we strolled the streets and cut down Broxton Avenue we did see a few busters from the Westside that would soon be enemies or dead—it was their choice; they just didn't know it yet. They were making some serious money out of this High End Pool Hall slash lounge on Olympic and Sawtelle and we wanted it more than they did. Shannon and Dez wanted the money and products but I saw the potential in the establishment. I wanted the deed to the property. They thought I was crazy thinking like that at 18 when I first brought it up but after I explained to them the value of property, they had addresses and pictures of parents and siblings ready to be kidnapped by the next day.

We showed them our best cowardly smiles and initiated the handshakes to make them feel like the tougher gang or whatever they felt like at the moment. All along, though, we were just sizing them up. A couple of them were cocky and looked at our ladies in a certain way 'cause they thought we were soft since we were playing the role. We made a mental note of that, fa-sho'. Those are the type of dudes that usually get slapped across the face in simple robberies. Acting is a tough job. We barely stayed in character.

We kept walking up Broxton Avenue window shopping and taking in the scene. We were having fun laughing and joking with Soncho and his lady arguing over some candy in her purse. She was petite with an appetite bigger than his. They had one piece of licorice left over from the movie so they decided to split it in half after they argued and wrestled over the purse for the past five minutes about who ate the most. Soncho playfully snatched the last piece of licorice out of Lu-Lu's hand and started running up the street half speed laughing. Lu-Lu trailed him and jumped on his back. She kept pretending to choke him until he gave up her half. He was still carrying her piggy back as they both ate each end of the licorice until they met in the middle and kissed. We fell out laughing. This big happy thug was a romantic at heart.

"Ain't that a bitch! That was some cute corny shit wasn't it?" Suge laughed and enjoyed the moment. Soncho and Lu-Lu were kissing with their eyes closed while she was on his back on a crowded street.

They were bumping into all the pedestrians passing by, which made it even funnier. One lady even fell down. I knew Soncho and Lu-Lu couldn't have caused that and that's when I heard a gunshot and frantic screams. We ducked for cover. I glanced up and saw some cats from one side running and their foes from the other side gunning for them. I saw the innocent victim lying there motionless. I wanted to help her, but there was nothing I could do. Even if she were alive, being who we were would have come down to a moral decision. In our hearts, we would have been doing the right thing but a gang killing of an innocent bystander in a white town, they would have put the blame on us just because. This was going to be bigger than a drive by shooting in South Central LA. This was going to have political ramifications. We had to flee like everyone else.

Westwood was never the same after that night. Like we figured. It got political. They implemented a 10 o'clock curfew law and were arresting kids by the thousands. From that, it didn't take long before people of all colors started going to jail all together. Independently owned businesses suffered. Corporations and chain stores moved in. It looks like a commercial ghost town now. The vibe feels totally different. All we have left are the memories of what Westwood Village used to be.

$ $ $ $

As I was driving to the hotel with my lady Toni, we didn't speak on what had just happened. We drove a few miles before I realized we were riding in silence. I had a tape in the cassette deck but I didn't remember what it was. I turned the volume up.

It was NWA. *"What about the girl who got shot, Fu—..."* I turned it off quickly before Eazy E finished his line. I loved that song but the timing was off.

Toni and I looked at each other as I said, "Yeah, that is not a very appropriate song at this point in time."

"Yeah baby that was awful timing. Not cool right now."

I put on Marvin Gaye and we said a silent prayer for the victim's family.

CHAPTER 12

FIFTY RACKS! That was a nice little come-up for a couple of minutes of work. But shit, once Shannon and I split it down the middle it didn't look as good as it did at first though we weren't complaining. We had a rule that when we strong-armed regardless if we got paid or not, as long as nobody got hurt or caught, it was a good day. If we got money or product, it was a lovely day.

Our little jack move didn't take too much elaborate planning. Matter of fact, it was more like improvisation. We ran into these young dudes from an up and coming hustlers crew just past the Palms area in west LA. They were young, hungry, and a little too eager. We met up with them in the alley behind the newspaper stand and the recently closed Millers Outpost Department Store off of Robertson and Pico. They wanted two keys of cola. Shannon and I were talking about all the work that went into breaking the product down, bagging all that shit up, and hitting the block to sell it. When we did it out of town, it was cool. It was worth the work and the risk 'cause we always came back with a grip.

In our backyard, we wholesaled. Yeah, we started off in the streets selling dope but unlike most dealers that had the story of doubling their first $50 bucks and evolving to a kilo, ours was slightly different. I jacked a nigga for my first Bird. Dez liked my tactics, too. Shannon would sell his some-timey customers stepped on shit when he needed to come up fast. He turned his ounces into kilos the hard way, but the trickery he learned along the way would help us all in the long run.

I was sitting in the passenger seat with two keys of cola in my lap.

We saw the nice little Toyota Celica pulling up the alley. Homie's car was nice. We could tell it was a graduation present. He didn't get that hustlin'. They were probably doing this for someone else or they were just turned on by the game. It happens. As the car approached, I looked out of the side view mirror and they were so happy to see us. They were definitely rookies. One of them got out of car with a duffle bag. Shannon popped his trunk from the inside. As homie was walking up, I clicked both keys together. All I saw was teeth his smile was so bright.

"Hey homie. I don't need to count that first, do I?"

"C'mon G, I wouldn't do that to you. I'm about my business."

"Okay, I heard you were a good dude. Toss the bag in the trunk."

Homie tossed the bag in the trunk and closed it. He slapped the metal and walked back to the passenger window still smiling.

"Is the bag in there?" I asked as I held up his merchandise to the window but I didn't I give him the product just yet.

"Yep!"

"Did you close the trunk good?" Shannon asked.

"Nice and secure," he answered.

I said, "Thank you."

And then we drove off.

Shannon looked in the rearview mirror and saw homie with his hands on his hips and mouthing the words, "Are you serious?"

$ $ $ $

So now we have two keys and $25,000 each. I was recounting the money in my room and heard my mama knock on my door. She didn't want shit. She just wanted to be nosey. Mama never told me not to do what I was doing but was always sneaking in my shit. That never made sense to me. She could have anything I had without question but for some reason she would rather sneak in my room when I was gone, break my door lock and lie and said I left the house phone locked in there or the iron or she couldn't find her cooking utensils or some far fetched excuse to go into my room. She opened my mail all the time and would say the mailman did it. She read personal letters from my girls and my diary when I was young. When I would confront her about it, she said she was being a good mother. That's the part I hated the most because that was so far from the Truth. My mama's mother was the same way with her. My aunts are the same way. It's a weak genetic defect. It never helps the relationships. It actually caused distrust and lack of respect.

"C'mon Mama, every time I come to my room to handle my business here you are trying to peak over my shoulder. There is nothing to hide. What's so fascinating about my room?"

"Nigga, this is my house. You pay the rent, but this is still my shit."

"This is the apartment you are leasing. I'm moving soon anyway, Mama. It's time for me to break anyway."

"Well, good!" Moms yelled. She didn't mean it. She was just mad that my door was locked. "As long as you're here, I ain't going to be talking to you through these damn walls in my own house!"

See, like I said: just nosey. It could be worse. Shannon's parents steal his money and use it on bullshit. Shannon has his own crib but he leaves money there since the days when Passion used to send Pirates there to rob his booty. That's why I had Shannon's half of the money in my safe. I packed my goodies in there, too, and shut it. I opened my bedroom door. Mama was standing there mad with attitude. She looked around my room, for what I don't know. I was moving soon as we came from this little trip back east we had planned. Mama was going to visit her sister in Richmond, CA, for a week a couple of days before we were leaving. She could have had a good five free days to go through all of my shit while I was gone in peace. I had guns, dope, and incriminating evidence in *HER* house and all she was worried about was my personal letters and whose panties I collected. That didn't make sense to me. She would make it known, "You have girls draws hid in your closet like some freak!"

I would ask, "What are you doing in the back of my closet anyway?"

"I was looking for the remote control to the TV."

"Way in the back of the closet, Mama? For real?"

"Well, that's where you hide everything else."

I couldn't wait to get my own crib.

$ $ $ $ $

Suge looked just like his name sounded. He was a fly-dressing, cute nigga. He was brown skinned, fit, with a dimple in his chin. Suge didn't have the pretty curly hair but he always kept a fresh cut. Suge loved to mack money and honeys, in that order. Even though he was a ladies man, he wouldn't make a great pimp. He doesn't like to be bothered with the same broad daily. It bores him. The girls he involved in the game were into credit cards and checks. He would get his ladies to date a baller from time to time so they could survey his layout so we could later rob they ass, but Suge didn't sell pussy or dreams. Suge claimed that he wasn't a gangster but if you brought it out of him, he was a different dude. If given the choice, he would rather handle business like a gentleman. Even if he had to resort to the murder game, Suge would rather stick a needle in their vein filled with rat poison or battery acid if time permitted over using a pistol. Guns were too messy and loud for his taste.

Suge lived in Brentwood. He came from money. His mother, Charlene Sugars, worked for Mayor Tom Bradley's office. They were always attending some $1,000-a-plate fundraisers. Suge's father died from emphysema when he was around 11 or 12. He was into selling commercial real estate. Mr. Sugars and Suge were tight. He left Suge with a nice sum of money, but he died before he taught him what to do with it. Suge took it real hard when his father passed. When we were youngsters, we saw Suge once a year at summer camp. After his pops died, we started kicking it almost every day for the past six years. I believe the death of his pops brought the dawg out of Suge. He was a smooth dude but he had a lot of anger and pain built up inside. He had no reason to bang other than being part of a brotherhood. He was already on the borderline in an outsider's eyes of being stupid for bangin' with a trust fund. They didn't know the demons he was fighting inside. Suge didn't feel like his father died; he had his mind made up that he was taken away. He felt robbed, raped, and purged. Suge did a good job keeping it inside. It was rare but when he snapped, he popped.

Dante was Suge's main man and crimey. They were both fly guys so it was inevitable that they bonded. Dante's father always made Suge feel welcome and he was appreciative but it wasn't his dad. The only time Suge and Dante ever got into a heated exchange was when Dante whispered under his breath like teenagers do that he couldn't stand his dad. Suge wished he had a dad to tell him to take out the garbage and he took offense. Besides that, they were like brothers. Dante always went with Suge and his mother to the Political Events. Dante went along to sell a little nose candy to the City officials, police, and clergymen that attended the gala affairs. We learned early that more people than we expected liked a little cocaine from time to time. Dante and Suge did find it weird that the politicians creating laws to lock us up for selling coke was using it freely among themselves like it was perfectly all right for them.

Mrs. Sugars had no interest in marrying again any time soon but that didn't stop the horny politicians from the City Council, the State Senate, and all those political offices from trying to get next to her. Suge smiled and shook their hands at the parties but he also gave them that *Don't even think about it* look. Suge wasn't going to block his mother's happiness but he wasn't going to let a married man that tricks with prostitutes use her or take advantage on days she is feeling lonely and vulnerable.

Suge and Dante were making some good easy money at those campaign fundraisers. It was too many judges and chiefs of police for me. They were given a pass to supply the party but at the same time, their names were instantly on their radar. But it wasn't because of what they were selling; they were more concerned that Dante and Suge knew their personal business and that they were capable of keeping their mouths shut.

$ $ $ $ $

"U Looze!" Dez barked as he took this fool's money that made a side bet while he was shooting dice.

"Seven! Give me that! …Seven! C'mon man, this is what I do, let me get that!"

"I didn't even see it, cuz. Stop picking up the dice so fast!" stated one of the angry baby locs that was losing his money.

Dice games in back alleys behind the store are very loud and aggressive. When a salty bad luck nigga loses his bread, it can get ugly at times. Dez was shooting craps in another set's hood, too. Fortunately, the cats that were losing were no threat to Dez. They were some Baby Locs from the Eastside but Dez did business with them. Even if Dez broke them, he would kick them back some change after the game just so they wouldn't get desperate and fuck off a package trying to come back up.

Noopy, Dez's homie from that hood, held him down over on that side of town. He was a shooter and his word meant something to the baby locs under his wing. His word didn't carry too much weight with the older OGs that weren't doing well in this new dope game. A lot of jealously and extortion tactics were used within the set. This new breed of gangsters adapted to the environment. The same OGs that we feared as kids walking home from school didn't look as tough once we came of age and learned what this new game was really about. If they were broke looking for a handout, they really got no respect. President Regan flooded America with coke. It was too much money on the streets to still be robbing liquor stores at 30 years old for a couple of hundred dollars.

Dez was breaking cats but he wasn't the only one winning. They had about 2Gs in cash laying in the pot on the ground. Two old niggas from the hood rolled up the alley in some raggedy bucket with a bad muffler. Soon as they heard the car that sounded like it was falling apart, the game paused immediately on instinct. It was Big Doodle Bug and some dude the baby locs didn't even recognize. Once we saw Doodle Bug's Jeri Curl, a few of his little homies threw up the set, and we resumed the game. They parked and got out of the car.

"What's up, you little muthafuckas? This is your big homie 1-Punch Knockout. He just got out of Folsom. He got sent up on a hot one when you little ugly bastards was still in diapers," Doodle Bug explained as he introduced us.

He didn't even have to tell them 1-Punch just got out, it was obvious. You talking about a nigga coming home on swole, his arms were every bit of 24 inches on the hang…. And his skinny legs were no bigger than some uncooked spaghetti sticks. He was towering over us standing a good 6'6" and looked like he didn't trust anybody in the world.

"I need y'all to welcome the homie home and put a little bread in his pocket to get him on his feet. He put in more work for the hood than all you little muthafuckas combined," Doodle Bug insisted.

The baby locs were only hesitant 'cause they were in the middle of a heated dice game. Their mind was on the action at the moment. Lil Scrappy spoke for the Baby Locs without ever taking his eyes off the game, "Hold up, big homie. We got you but we're doing something right now. Hold tight and we'll take care of you, big homie. Welcome home!"

A couple of the little dudes that were basically out of the game counted out 50 bucks between them and gave it to 1-Punch. I guess things worked differently 18 years ago when 1-Punch was terrorizing the streets because he took Scrappy's request to be patient a certain kind of way. 1-Punch KO walked in the middle of the dice game and picked up everybody's money off the ground including Dez's and started walking back towards the bucket.

Dez looked at Noopy since those were his homies to let him know he was about to take it there. Noopy gave him the go-ahead nod. Out came the strap.

"Hey homie," said Dez in a real cool voice. "I'm not from your hood and that's my money you're walking away with in your hand. Give me mines back and then whatever you do with the rest is between y'all."

1-Punch turned around and looked at Dez who was half his size. He started walking back towards him.

"All of this is my money, little nigga, and your life is going to be in my hands if you don't shut the fuck up and get out of my face!"

Dez got 1-Punch off parole two years early. He put one slug in the center of his forehead. Dez let off two more shots in the same spot for insurance as 1-Punch went splat in the alley.

OG Doodle Bug had ducked behind his raggedy bucket. He rose up with his 32 pointed directly at Dez's dome. But he didn't even get a chance to squeeze a shot off. Noopy started dumping on him until he dropped dead.

Doodle Bug was Noopy's big homie, but Dez was his employer and Dez paid him very well. Doodle Bug was more of a bill than a real Big Homie. The baby locs didn't really know how to take it. Doodle Bug was a nuisance but Dez wasn't from their hood. Before they could decide what was about to happen next, the shrill of sirens were in the air getting closer quick.

Noopy yelled to Dez, "We need to get up outta here! Let me get that heat! I'll dump them shits in the sewer. Let's move!"

$ $ $ $

Shannon, Dez, Soncho, Dante, and I went out of town at the perfect time. Suge had some shit he needed to handle in town but he was going to catch up with us when we got to New York. Khan didn't have his money right to roll. He didn't stack his bread. It comes in and it goes out. But this trip wasn't about making money. We wanted to play possum with that young hustling crew in Santa Monica. We had them thinking we didn't want any problems. They thought they had us punked. Once we returned to LA, we were coming back gunning for them.

We decided to go to Chicago and New York. For no reason other than it being popular and to say we did it. We had no ambition to set up shop in those locations. We weren't seasoned enough yet. We entered the city as tourists, but little did we know it was going to turn out to be real special indeed.

We roamed the streets of Chi Town looking at architecture that didn't interest us but we pretended like we were in the enchanted city of Atlantis or some shit like that. I don't remember what triggered the conversation but once it dawned on us that we were in the home of the notorious Al Capone, it captivated our attention. We even found an attraction in a traveler's brochure called the *Chicago Crime and Gangsters Tour.* We got pumped. The description said the tour was going to take us to the exact locations where Al Capone, Salvatore Giancana, Dean O'Banion, and other villains frequented, partook in illegal activities, and corruption.

Besides Al Capone we didn't know any of those other muthafuckas but Shannon did. He loved those old black and white gangster movies so he was up on game already. Shannon even knew where some of the locations were without the help of a guide. Shannon started telling us about the Holy Name Cathedral where an infamous shootout took place that left visible bullet holes in it. We bought tickets for the following day but Shannon swore up and down he was better than any damn tour guide. He conned us into taking trains and cabs to locations he was familiar with. Every place we arrived, the historic Gangster Hangouts Shannon bragged about on the way didn't physically exist any longer but they were the exact locations they once loitered. All we had to go on was imagination and Shannon interpreted stories. Shannon wasn't going to rest until he found something from the Prohibition Days.

"Shannon, you are worse than the lame ass nigga Illado Riviereo that had us watching him bust open Al Capone's vault for two hours on live TV and he didn't find shit!" I clowned Shannon about his tour guide techniques.

"I don't know what's worse, Illado looking like a damn fool on live TV or us looking like fools for watching that fool for two hours!" Soncho stated as he laughed at his own joke. We chuckled a little bit and looked at Shannon. He had us out there on a never-ending mission to nowhere for four hours. We were ready to shut it down and wait for the tour the following morning but Shannon was persistent. He just started asking every old ass muthafucka he saw on the street where Al Capone roamed. Most of the elderly people just pointed to places we had been already or they didn't know or cared to know.

A couple of slick cats in their mid-30s we saw walking with a diddy-bop up the street toward us tried to lead us into danger. They told us we needed to get the game first hand from Al Capone's right-hand man and all his Disciples in the Cabrini-Green Projects. If the one who was talking slick had told his sidekick to keep a straight face, he would have had us good. It was Sidekick's goofy snickering when he gave us directions that raised our antennas. The name of the area sounded familiar to me for some reason. I started thinking hard. I thought about the show "Good Times", the Chicago Bears; nothing rang a bell until I heard the L Train whiz by. That was where they filmed the movie *Cooley High*.

Thinking about when Cochise died in the movie rubbed me the wrong way. I looked at homeboy. I didn't trust him one bit. I said, "Thanks, homie, in advance, but I'm quite sure we'll be seeing you again."

"I doubt it," Sidekick stated and they both walked off laughing.

We did a little homework and learned the two busters were sending us to spot to be seriously injured. That was Gangster Disciple Hood or Territory or whatever they called their surroundings but I know we weren't supposed to be in it. Normally, we don't have problems with street cats in other states but we have never walked into a notorious project asking tourist questions either. Shannon was still determined. He was not leaving those cold Chicago streets until he found an old whiskey bottle from the Prohibition Era or one of Capone's cousins for some interesting conversation.

Dez started getting frustrated with walking on his tired feet all day in circles and coming up short. "Damn Shannon! Why are you so fascinated with these Al Capone hangouts? That muthafucka probably didn't even like Black people!"

"That's not exactly true, young fella. Al liked the color green, and if you had it and didn't touch his, he was all right. A little loud and obnoxious at times, lacked class, too, but he was okay for a Wop." We all turned around and saw this elderly Black man with a stern face impeccably dressed in an older model suit and Dobbs hat sitting at the bus stop. We could tell he had to be well into his 90s because of his voice inflection and he had developed that blue ring around his retina. He kept a neat handkerchief in his hand and wiped his wet mouth with it every few sentences. He still looked fit and fairly healthy. His cane was handcrafted and shiny but we didn't know if it was for walking or for style.

Shannon's face immediately lit up. "Hey Pops! Can you direct us to the clubs and speakeasies where all the mobsters used to hang out?"

"First off, I'm not your father. Everybody around here knows me as Pico Nikko and that's what I like to be called, you see? No Mr. Nikko, Old Man, or Pops. Pico Nikko. And now to answer your question, No! Hell no! What do I want to do that for? Those Capone Boys wasn't shit! They had the muscle and the complexion for the protection, you see? But if he was smarter and kept his dumb ass out of the papers he would have reached his full potential but it was cut short, you see? Let me ask you this. Why do all you Black kids fantasize about being Italian Mobsters and they were always trying to be like us?"

We didn't know what he was talking about. From what we gathered Black People only existed as Ex-slaves, Maids, and Butlers in the 1920s. We all had a puzzled look on our face. Pico Nikko looked at us and shook his head.

"You guys ever heard of a fella named Policy Sam?" We shook our head no.

"What about Teddy Roe?" We kept shaking our heads like we didn't have a clue.

Pico Nikko started running down a list of names. "What about Mush-mouth Johnson? Ike Sims? Royal Walker? I know you aware of whom Flukey Stokes is. He's running the town right now."

We stood there looking like five question marks.

"What about the Jones Brothers?" Pico Nikko asked and we shook our head no once again.

"Well gotdamn, y'all don't know shit! These are your own people, important people. Well, do you know Quincy Jones?"

We laughed 'cause we were happy we got that one right and told him yes.

"Well, he's from that Jones lineage, you see? These were the best gangsters that ever lived! Period! Those Italian mobsters were just gorillas you know, meaning aggressive. They didn't do business with style that garnered respect. Everything was by force and intimidation, which led to so many deaths in those days. You ever heard of a place called Bronzeville...the Black Metropolis-Where we lived in mansions, owned banks, controlled the politicians, built our own schools, hospitals and hotels… and unlike those tasteless Wops, most of our buildings are still standing today. Are you fellas driving?"

"No, sir. We are here from Los Angeles checking the sights," Dante answered politely. He was showing a whole new level of respect for Pico Nikko.

"Nigga, don't con me. Come here closer and let me smell you... Hmm, if you aren't out here to make money, then most likely you're playing possum on some punk crew moving in on your turf. I can see it in your eyes. In my day, you had to know shit like that to survive, you see? Chicago was rough coming up, man! Serious wickedness. Even young Quincy Jones, They tried to crucify him as a little kid. Some mean little muthafuckas nailed his wrist to a wall for fun. Its something else I see in your eyes I haven't seen in a long time— purpose! You are a different breed from these knuckleheads that's out here today. I try to tell these kids about their history and they don't give a shit. You fellas are attentive, you see. You can care less about a Mobster now right? You want to learn about these Jones Brothers now don't you? Well I'm going to school you… for a small fee. Can we agree?" Pico Nikko concluded and slide his fee in real slick like.

We agreed to his terms. He didn't want much and just the little information we got so far we were cool with that. Pico Nikko raised his cane and kind of shook it back and forth rapidly. A slick older model limousine peeled out from the curb across the street and made a U-turn to pick us up. This is the kind of vibe we were looking for.

Pico Nikko was the best tour guide ever. The stories he told were so good that the actual locations were just a backdrop to the information.

"This is where the great Teddy Roe allegedly killed this mobster hit man named Fat Lenny that was coming for him. The hit was ordered by this jealous bastard, uh what was his name?" Pico Nikko thought and snapped his finger a few times until he nailed it, "Sam Giancana!

Yeah, that shady muthafucka! I bet you heard of that asshole but never of Teddy Roe. Sam's outfit was trying to extort him for street tax, you see? But back then we controlled everything. Teddy Roe wasn't about to give up a cut of the profits to a bastard he wasn't doing business with. If he would have folded easy, they would have taken us all for soft, you see. Fat Lenny was what the Italians called a 'Made Man' and his brother was big time somebody, you see? Shit, Teddy Roe didn't see rank, he saw some white motherfuckers coming to kidnap him so he shot his fat ass. Under those conditions Fat Lenny was *made* for the grave. The ironic thing about Giancana, he would rather have a man like Teddy Roe than anybody in his organization. When the Feds was wiretapping his phone, the FBI had it in their you know the uh, (snapping fingers) um, not the police report, oh the transcripts, you see, Giancana said, *I'll tell you one motherfucking thing Black Man or no Black man Ted Roe went out like a man. This guy had balls. It was a fucking shame we had to kill a man like that.* You see?"

"So you're telling us there were Black Gangsters in the Prohibition Period that were living like Capone and Torrio and those guys. And wait a minute, that was the depression era, too?" I asked again because according to the history books we were one foot off the plantation.

"No disrespect to your friend here, but is he slow or hard of hearing?" Pico Nikko asked Dez as he tapped him on his bicep, and then he looked at me and continued. "Same as them? Man, we were living better. Teddy Roe lived in this mansion right up here on South Michigan Avenue. He had a couple of these bad boys. We all did. This home here is the one he hid out in when he was on the run for killing Fat Lenny, you see."

"He hid out in his Mansion? Oh, he was one of those *You have to come kill me* niggas. I like him. Please tell us he went down shootin'," Shannon said eagerly. I could see the wheels turning in his head. He was probably already thinking of a way to booby trap his pad if he ever got to this level. Shannon has an imagination that is wickedly great.

"Well young fella, not quite but they didn't get the best of him. Teddy could have gunned them all down but this was business—not a personal war, you see? Killing them all puts everybody at risk, you see?" He paused and looked out far away towards the sky. "In 1952, Teddy was diagnosed with terminal stomach cancer, you see. It was tearing his insides up. He only had a couple of months to live; you see Teddy was a prideful man. And back then they didn't have all that chemo shit. He didn't want to go out all sick and rotten. Teddy paid us all, you know the ones closest to him, a substantial amount of money to start a life, and then he told us to leave him be—all the security guys like myself, you know? He called a Wop he knew and disguised his voice and let him know where Teddy Roe might be. Man, he put on the best suit money could buy and started strolling down South Michigan Avenue, styling! Five Wops unloaded shotguns on him and he died with his back against this tree right here."

"I see now, sir. He went out like that to save face. The Italians looked powerful and business could keep moving. Even though we were Black with money we were still Black and didn't have the complexion for the protection. I got you."

Pico Nikko looked at me with a light in his eyes. He tapped Dez again and said, "Your boy ain't as dumb as I thought he was. You are going to be a good soldier young man if you keep your mind sharp… but yeah that is the legend of the great Teddy Roe paraphrased, you see? We would be here another five hours just talking about the funeral, so If I told you his life story we would be standing here for weeks and my legs are barely making it now. Lets get back in the car and take you to the areas where the magic happened."

As we drove down the streets of Chi Town Jimi Hendrix "Voodoo Chile Blues" started playing in my head, I was trying to picture visual images that related to the Pico Nikko stories. He had one for each block. But then there was one thing he said that caught my full attention.

"Teddy Roe was racking in 10,000 a day in 1938. By 1950, we were multimillionaires with generational wealth." Those words stuck to me for the rest of my life.

$ $ $ $ $

SluuuurrrrrrP!

"Mmmm, you taste so good! I love sucking your dick. The way it feels in my mouth, Mmmm Mmmm mmmmm! Ohhhhh sucking your dick makes my pussy so wet. Look at your dick baby... look at what makes my pussy squirt... ohhh sssss ahhhhh ssssss ahhhhh I want to feel it inside me now, wait let me like the head one more time Mmmmm ssssss ooohhh ssssssss! Ahhhhhhhhhhhhh! Ohhhhh yes-yes! It's that dick, baby! Oh yes!! Ahhhhhhhhh!" Suge was putting his Sweet-Sweetback in his Brazilian beauty Christiane and bringing the freak out of her. "Oh Suge! I'm cummin' all over your sweet dick already! I've never been with anybody that makes me climax so much and feel like this!" Christiane's screams of passion only made Suge's dick even harder. He was stroking it so good Christiane's eyes were rolling around in the back of her head like she was on the verge of blacking out. Christiane was riding his pipe something nice. She reversed her position and kept riding it with her ass facing him now. Suge couldn't see the color of his shaft. It was covered in Cream Pie ala mode. The pussy was great, but now it was becoming messy wet.

They put the sexual escapade on pause to freshen up and take a nice *chronic break*. Christiane had big plans. She was born in Brazil but her family migrated to the States to live the American Dream. Christiane was so pretty but she was so gangster. Her mannerisms and hustle proved she had a different agenda. If Christiane was one of those silly shit-starting types she could easily make men fight over her. She had nice sweet soft brown skin, long silky hair, round brown eyes, and the cutest good girl smile that was infectious. She has a slender figure that came with a sexy walk. She no longer had her accent but every now and then she would say shit in Portuguese that sounded sexy to us but it could have meant anything. Christiane was young when they moved here but she was already exposed to too much growing up in the Rocinha Favelas in Rio. The gangs run the Favelas, period. Sex is also a big part of that culture. Christiane enjoyed the art of fucking and making love. She had visions of creating a paradise for like-minded individuals that loved the art of sex like she did and she needed Suge's financial backing to fund it.

"It will be a place where all dreams come true. It will be magnificent, Suge. It will be an exclusive gentlemen's club. No brothel shit or skank massage parlors. This place will only cater to the elite love makers with a lot of money. I have the business plan already to go. I just need a strong man like you to partner up with that I can trust. You have what it takes. You were born with that gift to make women cream in their panties just being around you. Your beautiful smile, charming personality, and that dangerous element about you is so sexy. You have it all baby. I know you have your own hustle but pussy will sell when water won't."

"People have been calling me a pimp since I was a child, Christiane, even my own mother. Girls just like me and I like them. Pimping has nothing to do with being surrounded by a whole bunch of women that has a crush on me. Half the bitches that dig me are looking for a handout and the other half like me because I'm cute or some silly shit like that. These broads out here are not trying to make any money."

"Exactly, these lazy bitches in LA want you to hand them the world with nothing to offer in return but some dry pussy and a attitude. I'm bringing in the most beautiful women in from all over the world— none of these local bitches. Baby, nobody is going to pay top dollar for someone they can see everyday for free. These hoes in LA give you the pussy and ask for some money last… that's crazy. But before you say no, Suge, let me just show you the business plan and projected numbers. And in the meantime, let me give you a sample of what the clients will be receiving." She readjusted herself. "Mmm, I want it from the back this time baby, put it in right there, Mmm hmm that's it... Ssssssss Ahhhhhhhhhhhhhhh! YES!! That dick!!"

$ $ $ $ $

MEANWHILE BACK IN CHI TOWN...

"In 1941 alone our organization made 110 million dollars, you see. That's equivalent to about a billion dollars today. The policy racket collectively netted 25 million annually. The rest of our money came from legit investments, nightclubs, and the speakeasies, you see? We had our own banks, supermarkets, and car dealerships. We never sold one drug or even a drop of liquor during that time! State Street was for the Elite. We organized and was determined to leave the game with something if shit ever hit the fan, you see? .... I have a store, barbershop, and cleaners... that's all I need. I'm straight for the rest of my life and my children have something to inherit, you see?

Now like I said, you young men have that look in your eye I haven't seen in years. You are not taking me for an old fool just running his mouth. I've been involved in a lot of hustles, you know what I mean? A dear friend of mine out of New York named Whiz—I want you to look him up when you head out there if he ain't locked up again—boy, he's something else, but anyway... Damn I lost my point. Oh yeah! He warned me in the 40s that narcotics has different rules so be careful and know what you're doing in this game. You have to be good or it can go bad if you don't have the right people with you. Don't have people around you that want money in that game, have people with you that want to make money together. Remember this, too, especially in that narcotics business, you take some and you leave some, you see? You never take it all. Its OK to be wolves, Dez, but when you go out and kill, you have to come back and feed your pack, you see? The richer they see you, more fools are going to come gunning for you—the police, rival crews, girlfriends, wolves. I did my part the best I could but I know I could have done more with like-minded gentlemen around me. You see?"

That was all the knowledge we needed. All the other information he shared with us was just icing on the cake. Gangbangers in Los Angeles weren't even thinking on this level. We were so focused we wouldn't even know how to respond to a nigga asking us what set we were from. We didn't have time for the silly shit anymore. It was about to get real up in here. This was more than just being schooled by a true OG; Pico Nikko confirmed what was already in us. At least we know we are doing the right things in a raw dog world. We were definitely aware that the times have changed since Pico Nikko was in his prime but all his rules can still be applied.

Pico Nikko almost gave us an advanced course on politician control but we were not on that level yet, "How much is that Black Mayor Tom Bradley charging cats for turf out in Los Angeles nowadays?" Pico Nikko asked. We looked puzzled. We had no answer to that. He shook his head, not at us for being green but how much the game had changed. "I see you're not there yet but when you start making real big money you have to use your money to control these politicians. You got to have that nigga in your pocket! We'll talk about that later. Now, I'm going to give you a brief history on the Jones Brothers because you need to know this history, and then we are going to drop you gentlemen off. I have to meet a lady friend and tend to some grown man's business."

The Jones Brothers were some bad muthafuckas in their day according to Pico Nikko. It was three of them, I believe. I only remember one of their names—Mack, and I smiled because that's what they sometimes call me in the neighborhood. The similarities in the game usually start out the same but when it gets serious, that's when boys become separate from the gangsters. Just like most crews, the Jones Brothers started out small, running a number house out of the family-owned tailor shop. After a little flippin' and trippin' and clippin', they turned that penny game into a sophisticated empire. They weren't ballin' like cats in our era. They lived lavish and glamorous. The mansions in Chicago were nothing compared to the property they owned in other countries. They had villas on exotic islands before they had the name. They owned everything, Hospitals, Farms, Hotels, even schools but that criminal element they were involved in was always present. There were so many high profile death threats, corrupt police and politicians, extreme levels of violence that involved bombs and shit, and kidnappings were very prominent when the Jones Brothers were running the game.

"It was actually a kidnapping that exposed all the jealous muthafuckas to the money we were making, you see. Before then they didn't care what niggas was doing. When they found out we had big money, that's when it became a problem, you know what I mean? A little small crew of Wops kidnapped the eldest Jones brother and held him for ransom. Teddy Roe dropped them $100,000 to get his friend back, you see. They were making two million dollars annually by that time so we took the hit and paid that ransom. That's when being a Gangster started taking precedent over being a businessman. From there shit started going downhill fast. Because of jealousy, you see?"

Pico Nikko retuned us to the exact spot we met him. We gave him $1,500, $500 for the tour plus a grand slam for the valuable information.

"I knew you had it in you. You learned something today I see. Only the true gentlemen in this life get down like this. Knowing that I don't need this much shows me even more about your character. If you guys are smart, be careful, and stand by your principles even if it takes extreme measures to get your point across, you are going to get something out of this game. It's been a pleasure, my friends. God bless you."

Later on, old Pico Nikko took the money we gave him and handed out $50 bills to the poor people that needed it, not the ones that wanted it. That was another lesson we learned.

CHAPTER 13

WHEN WE ARRIVED IN New York, everybody immediately identified us with Harlem Cats. It caught us off guard 'cause we immediately assumed they were calling us Harlem Crips and took slight offense. We had no ill feelings towards those Crips, but we don't want to be called nothing else other than Westside Gangsters or Westside Macks depending on where you were at. That's all we heard coming out of the airport. "That's them young Harlem Niggas, they be gettin' it." "That's Harlem Cats right there. The Ultimate Swag."

We also heard one brother that knew we were from out of town say; "I think y'all need to tuck those chains until you feel the city out first and get settled in." We did as we were told not out of fear but because he said it sincere like a friend would and it was believable. Now don't let me lead you to believe we came to New York and we were so fly people stopped with their mouths open. Besides those youngsters nobody else gave a shit about us unless it mattered. They keep it moving out in New York.

Since we were labeled Harlem Cats, it was a unanimous decision on where we were staying. All we knew about New York was the Apollo Theater so that was our destination. We just wanted to tell our parents that we saw it. If we caught a show it would be even better. New York was a busy town. I liked the Hustle and Attitudes, but I couldn't live there. It was too dirty and crowded for a nigga like me. The cab we rode in smelled musty as a muthafucka and they had the nerve to not want to pick us up 'cause we were Black.

"We could never go cruising in our Low Riders out in this

muthafucka," Soncho stated like he was reading my mind.

"I was just thinking the same shit. All this noise and horn honking, and the traffic is still not moving? This is not cool at all. Hey Mr. Cab Driver, take us to the closest hotel to the Apollo Theater. Not a Luxury Hotel but not a Roach Motel either. Do you have any recommendations?" I asked the Cab Driver. I knocked on the bulletproof window and showed him a twenty-dollar bill before I placed it in the slit and slide it thru. The Cab Driver was a foreigner but from where? I don't have the slightest idea. When they said New York was a melting pot they were not lying. I'm quite sure we have more than Blacks, Whites, Asians, and Mexicans in Los Angeles, too, but I never see them muthafuckas daily and we live on the best side, which is the Westside. The Cab Driver had a thick accent from somewhere, but his English was very good.

"Hotel? I recommend you stay with a friend, buddy. The Roach Motel is our Luxury Hotel- 5 Star. If you want clean, buddy, you should go to Buffalo, New York. Its very nice up there," Cabbie suggested but we could sense it was more out of hustling us than him worried if we were in a clean and safe environment.

"Hell no! We ain't trying to go to gotdamn Buffalo! Man, take us to the Apollo. These muthafuckin' Mexicans is always trying to get over on a nigga," Dez said, as he got irritated all of a sudden from sitting in that musty cab in bumper-to-bumper traffic.

"He ain't Mexican," Soncho stated, which irritated Dez even more.

"Don't start no shit right now, Soncho. It's too hot in here. I ain't wit' all that shit anyway. Its Blacks, Whites, Chinese, and Mexicans. That's it! Fuck it!"

"I'm Albanian, sir. I'm from Albania."

"See what I'm saying? Mexican!!" Dez stated as he got his point across.

"I can get you to a hotel, but I recommend you find some friends and stay with them. The price is not worth the risk of admission, buddy. It's not dangerous. It's just not always the cleanest. I thought you guys were from here. You look like you are from Harlem with your nice pretty clothes on."

"That's what everybody keeps saying," Shannon interjected.

"What's happening in the other boroughs?" I asked.

"Manhattan keeps on making it, Brooklyn keeps on taking it, Bronx keeps creating it, and Queens—well ,you know the rest, right? Money Making Manhattan, Harlem Uptown, that's where you belong, you can wear your jewelry outside, the minks, and the furs. Brooklyn sometimes called Crooklyn- Bed-Stuy Do or die –Brownsville; never ran; never will. They will strip you naked for $40 bucks. Be very careful in Brooklyn…" This muthafucka cabbie was trying to sound hip. He reminded us of this cat named Farooq that worked at Burton's Clothing in the Fox Hills Mall.

"Damn, you make it sound like normal people don't live there," Soncho said.

"They don't. Brooklyn is its own planet with its own set of rules. You can't wear sandals on hot days. Poor kids can't play and get dirt on their sneakers or they get beat up. Its crazy! Stick up kids is everywhere. I never drive my cab to Brooklyn. I got robbed eight times by the same little guy with two big guns."

Traffic finally started moving. The horns didn't stop honking but we were making progress. I could see the shift in cultures as we rolled down every block. We arrived at the Harlem Astoria Hotel. We tipped the cab driver and sent him on his way. It was everything a cheap motel in LA would look like, but with luxury hotel prices. The rooms smelled stale but they were decent. We weren't about to pay for five rooms like we planned. We said fuck that and put up $25 a piece for one room. They gave us extra cots and everything. New York didn't give a fuck about occupancy rules. We definitely liked that aspect of it. They suggested it actually.

It was a nice warm day, not too hot and humid. We freshened up and hit the Harlem streets in our freshest LA summer wear. We wore assorted colored Izod Lacoste Tennis Short Sets and Fila BJ Short Sets down to the matching socks. But we all rocked the white K-Swiss fresh out of the box. We rocked our sport watches, nice elegant neckpieces, and bracelets. We never wore gaudy jewels. Our jewels were solid gold, small but carried a lot weight.

We liked Harlem. We could see why people thought we were from there. It was a fly town. Now my boy Dez, if he were from New York he would be a Brooklyn Nigga for real. He was a taker. The first thing we noticed was everybody our age walked or rode the train. We got directions to the Apollo Theater and made our way to 125th Street. We probably took 100 pictures at one location. That was all we needed. We didn't know any other Black Landmarks. We asked around about Whiz, the old dude Pico Nikko wanted us to look up but somebody said he got flagged off for some reason or another. We kept posing for pictures until the film ran out.

"Y'all taking pictures like you never seen the Apollo before, damn!" said this sexy around the way girl named Renee. She was fresh to death. Her friends were nothing to ignore either. As they got closer to us ,they could detect something was slightly different about us.

"Wait, I thought y'all was somebody else. You remind me of these dudes that work for Slick and Jaybo. Y'all from around here?"

"No, sweetheart, we're from LA," Dante spoke for us. "What's your friends' names? Go ahead and introduce us with some Harlem hospitality."

"This is Roxy, Shanti, Toi, Keelee, and I'm Renee. You guys look like the niggas from around the way… except him," pointing at Dez. "He has a Brooklyn demeanor."

"How you think LA niggas are supposed to look?" Dez asked with an aggressive tone."

"You know, Jeri Curls and shit, we thought you niggas was Bama,"

Keelee said with no shame and laughed.

"So what's crackin' out here? You got a hooptee?" Shannon asked. He did not want to ride the subway.

"Oh yeah, y'all definitely ain't from out here. I can tell by the lingo. You hear it now, girl?" Renee asked her friends.

"Yeah, I hear it. But they look like them niggas up on St. Nick. They'll blend right in," Toi added.

"Well that's where we are headed. Roxy and Shanti are going to meet their dudes on 145th and St. Nick. You're more than welcome to come with us. We just hang out and talk shit. Everything is cool. Most of the people over there are in those streets but it looks to me like that's your type of crowd," Renee said matter-of-factly.

"And what type is that?" Shannon asked.

"Fly niggas that be gettin' it. That type! Am I correct or did I mistake you for some customers?"

"I don't like the way that shit sounded. *Customer* that sounds too much likes Buster," Dez stated with anger.

"No disrespect. So y'all want to roll or what?" Roxy asked.

"Yeah we down. Let's roll. …damn, we have to walk?"

$ $ $ $ $

When we got to 147th and St. Nick, let me tell you like this: Action, Energy, and Drugs are synonymous with that area. The energy we felt was unreal. There were no loitering laws like in LA. Everybody was hanging loose and doing the damn thing; it was all about money. They were trying to have some or trying to get some.

"Oh these niggas is doing too much out here. But I likes this shit," Soncho stated as he saw multiple cats flashing bankrolls and jewels.

"They are doing the most." I noticed as well. Everybody took notice when we strolled up. They all did a double take, then looked down at our sneakers. We had the same flavor but the shoe game is what separated us. They wore a lot of Fresh Shell Toe Adidas and Nike Cortez. I know they were feeling our fresh K-Swiss. We had them sitting right on our feet with the colored Izod and Fila socks. It was two dudes that immediately stood out from the crowd. They were our lookalikes as far as style. They had sport cars, just like we had back home. We were all wishing we had our rides. On foot, we were missing the most instrumental tool in the arsenal. This has nothing to do with confidence or lack of it because of materialistic items. This was some fun friendly competition on some fly shit. They were immediately drawn to us to us as well. We all made direct eye contact. Usually we would be sizing up Hustlers like these, and I'm quite sure they would be doing the same. But we were checking each other out on how we were styling. I saw the darker one with the slick Bucket Hat lean over to his homeboy and whisper something to him. He probably asked if he knew us.

Renee was looking at them watching us and vice versa and she said, "Y'all gear is on point. Harlem niggas are the Flyest in New York so for you to catch the Mayor of Harlem's eye, then y'all definitely got something going."

"Which one is the Mayor of Harlem?"

"Both of them. It's really three of them, but Hazz never comes out much. They are all the *Mayor of Harlem*. That's Slick and Jaybo, the dudes I thought y'all worked for. I told you y'all had similar styles. Did I lie?" Renee asked, but it wasn't a question.

We nodded in their direction and the one named Jaybo flashed the biggest, most infectious smile I'd ever seen on a Gangster. That dude had a beautiful spirit, but those are the most dangerous. We smiled back. Then Jaybo gave us another kind of smile and we had an idea what that meant. We weren't going to back down either. We were ready for the shit to jump off later on that night. Jaybo nodded his head in admiration towards us a few more times along with that big, beautiful smile that made us want to be his friend. He hopped on his motorcycle and hit a wheelie down the block, turned around, came back up the block doing the same wheelie and threw up about $5,000 dollars in the crowd. The cat Slick hopped in his BMW and peeled out in the opposite direction. We looked at each other.

"You know they coming back and we're going to see them later on?" Shannon stated as he gazed down the street following Jaybo's exit.

"I know. You know what we got to do," I agreed.

"It's some bad bitches over there. I'm trying to have me one," Dante noticed as he tapped Dez to get his attention.

"It's dead over here. Let's go over to Willie Burgers," Renee suggested.

We looked around and it was poppin' to us like this was the block to be on.

"It looks good to us."

"That's cuz you looking at pussy. It's more at Willie Burgers that's not taken. All those bitches are with somebody. We only came here so Roxy and Shanti could get some money from they niggas. They'll catch up to us later. Let's go to Willies," Renee said and led the way. As I checked out all the local hustlers I can see they were serious.

"Hey Renee, can you suggest a good place to go shopping?"

$ $ $ $ $

When we got to Willie Burgers, it was just like being in Westwood but full of hustlers. It was so many different things going on at one time it was like an amusement park for money. We saw hoes, fools buying blow, some just hanging out and talking good shit, and couple of dice games that we immediately wanted to be part of, especially Dez. Dudes were holding fistfuls of money and we wanted some. This was the first time we were comfortable pulling out our bankrolls with confidence.

We stuck our head in the game and became thoroughly disappointed. They were playing a game with three dice called Cee-Lo. We were like *What the fuck is this shit?* I mean, dice are dice and let them fall where they may, but the odds of some hood niggas explaining the rules correctly while they're gambling with all that money on the ground were worse than us playing green and blind. We studied how they got down and asked a few questions here and there before we got involved.

From what we gathered, our usual 7 or 11 was not a winner in this game. 4-5-6 was the magic number. 1-2-3 was equivalent to crapping out. Hi and Lo Trips and Points were also pretty simple to pick up on fast. The variants of the game like *Fevers, Loose rolls or Sloppy dice, Ace out, and Catch-ups* was too much to grasp in a hostile environment gambling with up big money.

It was too much money out there not to try though. We started taking side bets. We put our money on who had the hot roll. In New York, you can make a side bet on anything. They will bet how many times a roller will shake the dice before he rolls. It was big action on anything. We made some money and we lost some money, but we enjoyed the gambling and talking shit. We met a lot of cool muthafuckas. They were more like characters than regular people. They had big personalities. They were funny, too. When it came to playing the dozens, those dudes don't let up. We called it baggin' but they called it snappin' and they had jokes about that. They were very passionate about their rap, too. They were naming New York rappers we never heard of.

We kept hearing about this club called The Rooftop. It sounded like the place to be. They said something about a joint called the Latin Quarter, too, but The Rooftop was where everybody said they were headed that night. They were going to meet back at Willie Burgers first, then head to the club. They stressed the importance of meeting up first. We were all in. It didn't feel like they were setting us up at all. They were very hospitable. Once they found out where we were staying offers poured in from friendly strangers saying we could stay with them. They are very anti-Hotel in New York. We put a few offers we were willing to accept on pause just in case we lined some pussy up later on. We already paid the Hotel for the night but we were definitely shaking up out of there the next afternoon regardless.

"I like these Harlem Cats. I've never felt so comfortable around so many killers without my heat. I wish I had it though and my car but I feel safe *in the sense* that we aren't attracting enemies that's jealous because of our style. You know, I got to be specific around Dez and Shannon," I said.

"You got that right. I don't trust nobody in the game outside of y'all. The key word you used was killers. All those fools we were gambling with had guns. They weren't holding them to match their outfits. They prepared just in case some shit jumps off. I ain't about to get caught out here without some heat now that I saw that," Dez reiterated.

"What you talking about? We left our heat in LA. I know you didn't bring your heat on the plane!" Soncho asked, confused.

"Keep your eyes open, Soncho! They were selling everything from dope to subway tokens out in that bitch. Me and Shannon got a couple of 4-5's. Homeboy said he had to hit a couple of niggas with them but they lived. It ain't no bodies on them so he gave em' up at a cool price," Dez said, scolding Soncho for not being more attentive to his surroundings.

"I got me a Deuce-deuce new from homie that looked like he was from that movie *Beat Street* with the Kangol Hat, Big Glasses, and no shoelaces in his Adidas," I stated nonchalantly.

"Damn! All I got was a knife! One dude tried to hit me with a piece with duct tape around the handle. I knew a hot one was on that shit," Dante stated pissed off.

"Y'all didn't get me one? Man, y'all some dirty niggas," Soncho said sadly as he put the blame on us.

"Just stay close nigga, you'll be all right," Dante laughed.

"Fuck you, scandalous selfish assholes."

$ $ $ $ $

Shannon stopped at a phone booth and called his brother collect. Shannon figured since he was paying the bill anyway it didn't matter. His Moms still bitched about it, too. I guess parents still have to feel in charge even when they are no longer paying the cost to be the boss. I remember our parents saying when we start paying bills then we could do what we want. They did not expect us to start making more money than them a short time later. That old quote came back to bite them in a big way.

"What do you mean, you fucked up?" Shannon began yelling in the phone immediately after saying hello.

"I made the drop, counted the money out but when I got home like $10,000 was missing. I don't know where it went."

"Who were you with?"

"The homie Eric but he didn't have noting to do with it," Khan spoke honestly and in shame.

"I'm tired of you fucking up. If you weren't my brother, boy, I'd be taking you for a long ride in the trunk. You already owe me damn near $40,000 from fucking up the last three times. What the fuck is wrong with you? Blood or not you are going to make up that money and I want it by the time I get home."

"C'mon Shannon! That would mean I would be on the block working all day," Khan said as he showed his laziness was the reason the money was always short.

"You damn right! Get out on the block or whatever you got to do and get my money!"

"C'mon Shannon..."

"I ain't listening. Bye!" Shannon hung up the phone heated. But just like that, Shannon was back to his regular old stubborn self and ready to go shopping.

If we were back home, we would be able to feel out the spot we were hitting and dress for the occasion. These Harlem natives are serious about their fashion. We were going to have to spend a little bread since we didn't have all our tools to make a splash. Shannon was the first dude in our crew that took chances with fashion. He won't hesitate to wear something a gangster nigga may find non-intimidating as long as the bitches liked it. He'll tie a Polo Sweater around his neck and play the country club look often. He'll let you tease him about it and everything but just don't give him a reason to take it off. Shannon was up on this store called Bergdorf's. It was expensive but they had the shit we needed to succeed. Shannon had a wonderful eye for piecing his outfits together. My thing was soft, elegant fabric. The quality of the material is what caught my eye. We ended up shopping for shit to take back to LA. We forgot all about what we originally came there for. They had Ralph Lauren outfits that would never make it to Los Angeles. We bought a lot of that fly shit. When the salesman told us he would work a deal since we were buying together. We began to love New York even more. We would have been paying more for sales tax, department store tax, and mall tax than the outfits we were trying to buy in Los Angeles. This was our kind of town. They get down to business.

We put together fly shit for the evening, you know, some *For Business or For Pleasure* type of outfits for the occasion. We didn't want to do too much, but just make it known we were some fly muthafuckas, too. We dropped about three to four grand apiece. We wanted more, but we needed a car. Carrying the bags we accumulated between us on top of trying to get a cab was looking fucked up already.

Once we got outside, it was worse. We look like tourists doing too much. A BMW 725 and a stock Benz rolled up on us. A thick, brown skin nigga we recognized from the 3-Dice Game named Chips stuck his head out of the window of the BMW. "What's good, Cali cool cats? Where's your ride?"

"We're trying to get a cab back to the hotel. How come these muthafuckas won't stop for us?" Soncho asked, irritated. We triggered something again. I don't know what it is with New York hotels but Chips got so offended I thought I let my Father down.

"Get in the car, man! You staying at a fuckin' Hotel? Put your bags in the car, man, and let's go get your shit. Y'all staying at my crib, man, and I'm not taking no for an answer. This is ridiculous!" Chips called out to his man driving in the Benz, "Hey Jerzy, let two ride with you, man. They are staying at a fucking hotel. God! Let's go get their shit, man. This is fuckin' crazy!"

"We're only here for one more day," I said to let them know we wouldn't be a burden.

"What? Let's get your shit, man. I don't give a fuck if you were staying twenty weeks or twenty minutes Sun. Get all your shit, man. You ain't staying in no fucking hotel. Nigga, this is Harlem! Fly niggas take care of fly niggas. C'mon man, let's go get your shit, man. You ain't staying in no fuckin' hotel. Man, get your shit and get the fuck outta there. If it ain't enough room in my crib, I'll go stay with my bitch and you can have my room… C'mon man, let's go get your shit and get the fuck outta there, man!" Chips went on and on.

We never said no. We never declined his offer. Our mind was made up that we would stay at his pad, but regardless, he never gave us a chance to say OK. We let him vent. He was so damn passionate about it we thought, *Fuck it. Let him get it off his chest.*

"C'mon, man. You going to take your new pretty clothes to a dirty ass hotel? Get the fuck outta here, man! Go get your shit man. Go get all your shit and get the fuck outta there…" We heard that shit all the way to the hotel and after we left the hotel until we got to his pad. He just changed a few of the verbs around.

"You got your shit outta there? OK. Now you coming with me, man. You got all your shit now, you rolling with me, man! This is how we get down...You in Harlem, man! Y'all smoke? I'll grab some Phillies."

"What's a Philly?" we asked. "We smoke straight weed but no more funny shit laced in it." Then Soncho told him what we preferred because he was having flashbacks when we experimented with those white boy drugs at his crib and it turned into a cold-blooded orgy.

"We smoke in cigar wraps out here. I'll get you some of those white papers though."

"Yeah, Zig Zags in the White Pack."

$ $ $ $ $

We got to his building and we almost had second thoughts. It wasn't the projects, but it was huge and a gang of units in that bitch. If we were back home, it would look like... The Projects. The elevators smelled pissy and the hallways reminded us of a school building but the inside of his crib was extra fly. It felt like we stepped into a different world. Chips had his pad laid out. His taste in custom furniture was excellent for a young cat. It sported style and substance. He taught us something about ourselves. We had the cars money and clothes, but our crib game was on a rookie level. Shannon just had a couch and a bed at his crib. I still lived with Moms and slept in my same twin bed I had all my life. Chips had art on the walls, hand carved wooden animals on the mantle, sleek flat tables, and exotic plants. It was some fly living.

Chips saw the admiration in our eye and jumped on the opportunity. "Hey. I'm quite sure you know I get down in these streets, but I do modern interior design, too, you know, for home and office. So if you know of any of those Hollywood movie stars out your way and can put a word out for me, you know, a commission is coming your way without question. Let me give y'all my card."

We had big Kool-Aid grins on our faces. We were looking at a real live street nigga with a hobby. It was one of those moments that triggered a warm laugh on the inside. Chips could sense the adulation and smiled, too, out of sense of pride.

"Hey man this is Harlem. This is how we get down. We sell commodities. If it ain't nothing out, there we create something, baby! We use natural resources very well. Just because I'm making good money on this coke didn't put me in the class of being a born hustler; I came up carrying groceries for old ladies to actually working in the store 'cause they recognized my hard work. I went from bagger to cashier up to manager so when we came of age and got ready to rob that muthafucka I knew the whole layout of the store top to bottom… Now I own a store, with theft insurance," Chips told us and we fell out laughing. We liked Chip's hustle. He was a real good dude. He was serious about those streets too. He didn't even have to talk about it. He had the eyes of a wolf but a heart of an angel. This was New York; every walk of life is present, spiritual and metaphysical not just races.

$ $ $ $

We couldn't wait to roll up to Willie Burgers. We were stylin'. We looked the part. We wore a variety of designer shirts, pants/jeans, jackets, soft leather Cole Haan loafers or boots and was doing the damn thing. These Harlem Cats are Fly—ain't no doubt about that— but they couldn't match our swag. If they were Fly, we had Wings then and were ready to soar. Chips had rolled out earlier and we told him we would get down there on our own. Its something we liked about that exciting energy we got walking in that St. Nick area. It felt better than Christmas, that's for sure. In the three to four hours that passed since we were there last, it seemed like we lived there. People were either calling us by name or saying, "If you're Chip's folks, you must be good people. That's all he fucks with. If you need anything fam, we got you! Anything, fam; it's all love out here!" We heard that up and down the block. That shit felt great. Dez and Shannon were pessimistic; they didn't believe it could be love in the streets that was real. It had to be something to it. They couldn't trust something they've never seen before. LA Hustlers are Capitalist and Independent Contractors. We don't organize and pool resources together. It's a learned practice. We are not good at it but we're learning early so Dez had the right to view the streets from his eyes to survive.

When we got to the burger joint, we all started to get the sense that we were being set up. The vibe was different. We felt it from fifty yards away. The joint was packed. The sense of walking into danger entered our minds but we kept moving towards it because there weren't any threats. It was something else. They were prepared for our stylish arrival. All eyes were on us, but the faces had no frowns.

In an instant, the crowd kinda opened up and we could see those cats Slick and Jaybo in murder mode and dressed to kill. We were doing our thing, but they showed us what that custom tailoring game was all about. All of us were young with money and could buy the same expensive shit so we were still on even playing ground and no winner can ever be declared from that. So it didn't matter how much money we spent on our clothes; it came down to how we were rockin' it. That's when those New York Cats got serious.

Let's start with the brand new sports cars, fresh off the showroom floor. I had to start there because their clothes matched their cars. The Jaybo cat had these rust colored boots on called Timberlands to match the custom Louis Vuitton jacket he had on—now that was cold-blooded. They all had on fresh sets of jewelry that matched the cars and the clothes. These young cats were clean. Jaybo flashed that big smile at us, jumped in his ride and vanished. He had put on a show and did the damn thing.

As we looked around the crowd, everybody was dressed to the

nines. We searched for clothes we think nobody else is wearing and do a pretty good job. But custom outfits made specifically for you leaves no doubt that nobody else has it.

Now the ladies were on a whole 'nother level. It was easy to detect by their attitudes which ones were the main ladies and which ones were trying to disrupt their happy home. That was a huge difference in between East Coast and West Coast: those New York hustlers spoiled their women. Whatever they wanted, they could have it.

We did not get down like that on the West Side, player. If a special lady was down for the game, whatever we had they had. If we go shopping for an event, we might get them something, too, under certain conditions. We have a great time and do it big all on us, but no cash handouts. We don't do the hair and nails shit and *can I have* talk on the Westside. We like independent bitches that got their own hustle or may need a little help getting one going. We buy them something nice 'cause we wanted to from the heart, not to buy our way into some pussy. That's where the game gets fucked up.

But checking out those New York bitches and the way they styled their diamonds and designer outfits made us consider taking on that bill. Those bitches were bad. They looked liked they were supposed to have all those luxury items placed upon them. They earned it. A lot of the LA bitches we fuck with don't have the desire to do what it takes to wear those diamonds and furs. They want you to just give it to them. Don't get it twisted; bitches are the same everywhere, they just come in different forms.

"What you and your friends up to?" said this fine broad with thick eyebrows and street toughness about her. She had a few friends with her and all of 'em was decked out in the finest hip-hop fashion from Bloomingdale's. They had a feminine toughness about themselves as well. They were attracted to Dez more so than the rest of us. Chips told us to beware of fly Brooklyn hood rats that ran in packs. It seems as if we had managed to stumbled upon some.

"What's up? Y'all down with the Mayors and the rest of those niggas? We ain't never seen y'all around here before," the thin chick named Mona with extensions in her hair, gold rings on every finger, and ten gold chains around her neck asked.

"Yeah, something like that, but we in town for a week from LA. We staying over at the Harlem Astor. Why don't y'all come through and show us some New York Hospitality?" I lied to see where their head was. Shannon didn't care where their head was at as long as his *head* could get licked on.

"I want the one in the crew that's sucking dick."

"Damn, nigga! That's how you go about it. That's all you're looking for?"

"Yeah, we're in town for a week and I'm ain't trying to get married. I want some head. You in the game; I don't have to sugarcoat shit. You not the one I want anyway. So why are you talking? Point me to the one that's down for sucking on some dick tonight."

Four of the girls stepped back and looked in the direction of the known *dick sucker* of the crew and started laughing. She rolled her eyes at them and laughed it off. The one that seemed to have a problem with it spoke up though. She liked something about Shannon's brash attitude. She pressed her body up against him and said, "How do you know I ain't the one you want? You didn't ask me."

Shannon looked at her lips and the way her mouth moved. He looked over at the fellatio expert's full lips and wide tongue and said, "Cuz she's the one I want right there. She's a freak."

Baby Girl rolled her eyes and walked away from us. Her friends stayed and we got well acquainted with them. We could have had better choices, but they made it easy.

$ $ $ $ $

"Hey Santana."

"Hey baby girl, what's good? You doing your homework and

gettin' the drop on those mayor niggas in Harlem?"

"It's taking a little longer than we thought. They have their choice of bitches so we have to play this cool or they going to know something is up. We have to be patient on that lick. But in the meantime, I got fresh food for y'all to eat if you're hungry."

"My stomach started growling soon as you mentioned food. Who's the marks?"

"These weirdo GQ looking muthafuckas from LA. They're some clown niggas, too. They out here naked, flashing a little money, all jeweled up in that expensive shit."

"Some LA niggas? And they're not tooled up? Are they here on vacation or what, shorty? How many of them is it?"

"It's four of them. They act like they working with the Harlem crew but they out here tricking for pussy. They are staying at a hotel so that tells you they don't have any real folks out here. I already pressed up on the biggest trick in the crew and got him for his hotel key. They each got about four G in their pockets, plus jewelry. You can take these soft niggas down with one gun and a driver. You don't even need the Brooklyn Zoo."

"Good work, baby girl. You know what you doing and how to play this. You ain't no rookie. Hit me on the hip after you get them feeling comfortable. Get them naked and tickle their balls for a little while. If they our chumps like you say, I'm just going to make this a two-man operation. I'll be waiting on your call. One.

"All right, baby I'm holding you down. One."

$ $ $ $ $

The Rooftop was poppin' and we met plenty of chicks that were better suited for us to continue having a good time but Shannon was so adamant about getting his dick sucked so he kept those Brooklyn bitches close to us. Chips and his crew took care of us all night. They loved spending money and showing folks a good time. If they had access to better quality weed in the hood, New York would have easily become my favorite town to visit. My wheels started turning when they copped us some dime bags. The quality and quantity was shitty. If I could get a hundred pounds of that good LA shit out here, I could come up with a loyal cat like Chips holding it down.

"Y'all got rubbers in your hotel room? If not, we can stop by the store. I need some more gum anyway," Bridgette said, looking for an excuse to make it near a phone so she could call her goon squad.

"You got the other key to the room right, Shannon? I'll roll with Bridgette to the store and y'all can go on ahead of us. I got my key," Dez suggested.

Shannon was tipsy and horny. He checked his pockets several times and patted his body down to where there were no pockets at all and said, "I don't have it. I think I lost that little muthafucka. I can't find it. I must have left it up in the room or something. Just give us yours and we'll meet you in the room." Shannon started walking toward the Hotel with Thick Lips before he finished his sentence well. Dez tossed him his key.

Dez went the other direction to the store with Bridgette. Before they go to the store door, Bridgette said, "Go ahead on in and get the condoms. I have to call my Auntie's house and check on my baby."

"Oh yeah, you have a baby? What do you have? A boy or girl?" Dez asked just for general conversation.

"I have a little girl named Brittany. She's two years old." Bridgette lied so well. She would be the perfect bitch to have if she ever had to hit the witness stand for her man.

"Oh yeah, those terrible twos; I heard it was something else," Dez said as he walked into the store.

"Yeah… something else," Bridgette smiled and kept the façade going. Then under her breath, she said, "That's a nice polite-ass nigga; we gots to get him." And then she made her call to the Brooklyn Zoo.

"...See you in exactly one hour. This is easy money!! One!"

Bridgette entered the store and saw Dez putting a few items he purchased in his jacket pockets.

"I already paid for your gum. You just have to pick out your brand."

"Thanks… gimme that DoubleMint right there. I don't want that old shit you got at a discount from Halloween. I know how you *A-Rags* get down. I want that pack right there, sand nigga," Bridgette said rudely as she pointed. The cashier looked at Dez.

"Hey man, I'm just visiting, you have to deal with that daily."

"Fuck both of y'all!" Bridgette stated and rolled her eyes at the both of them.

She grabbed Dez by the bulge in the front of his pants and led him out the door. "Come on!"

$ $ $ $ $

"What I want to know, bitch, is are you gonna suck it or not? Shit, my dick is hard as a muthafucka!" Shannon was woofing while he stood in front of Thick Lips' face with his dick out solid as a rock.

"I don't wanna do it all in front of them, we ain't got no privacy, damn!"

"Bitch, we about to have a orgy up in here. We all in one room. What you think we all gonna do stand outside and take turns on the bed. Fuck all that. You knew what time it was when you got here. So let a nigga get some head. You letting a good hard dick go to waste. Didn't your mama tell you about wasting good food? Listen to your mama now and enjoy this choice beef."

"I don't eat red meat," Thick Lips snapped back.

"Aw, just relax, Shannon. She ain't the only bitch in here that wants to suck that big ass dick. Why don't y'all take off them clothes and let's get this party started," Mona said as she started undressing. She was skinny but she had some nice big brown titties. They sat up just right, too. When she dropped her pants, she had a nice gap. She looked good in her panties. They made her pussy look pretty. She came over and sat on my lap and started grinding on me. She put my hands on her exposed breasts and started moving my hands in the direction that turned her on the most. She reached her right hand out and grabbed Shannon's dick real tight. She started jacking it off real hard. I threw Mona off my lap and got the fuck out the way. Shannon's dick was too close to my area and he's scandalous enough to bust a nut near me. He wasn't fool enough to blast one on me even as a practical joke 'cuz he knows I would kill that muthafucka with my bare hands if he did some shit like that. But I still wouldn't put it past him.

We all got asshole naked and paired up with the chick we wanted to fuck over first.

"Hey Dez, you got those rubbers?" Soncho asked 'cuz it was no time like the present to set it off.

"Yep!" Dez walked across the room, full erection, over to where he hung up his jacket. He dug his hands in both pockets, pulled out four guns, and tossed them to us.

"Y'all bitches got us confused with some niggas that never seen some hood rats set a muthafucka up before. Get your asses up and get in that gotdamn bathtub!" Dez ordered and tossed us the duct tape he bought from the store. The look on those bitches' faces was priceless. I would have paid money for a snap shot. They weren't scared or nothing like that, just in shock that we were a tad bit slicker.

We all stayed naked until we taped and bound them set-up bitches together until the both rolls were gone. We tore their blouses in strips and gagged their mouths shut. We placed those broads in the bathtub stacked on top of each other as uncomfortable as possible and they was looking like duct-tape mummies. We got dressed quickly. We actually wanted to wait and surprise the niggas that were coming to rob us so we could rob them, but we didn't know how many were coming. We just knew it was the Brooklyn niggas we were warned about. We forgot to quiz the bitches before we taped their mouths shut and we weren't about to do it now so we robbed those broads for their money, jewels, and the DoubleMint gum. Putting a murder down didn't even cross our minds. If the shoe were on the other foot, we would have had our hood rats do the same thing so it was honor amongst thieves. One other coastal difference that came to play was we left them their clothes. If they had caught us like that, they would have taken everything down to the shoes and socks. We didn't want to take their self-esteem, just a little bling and green. We packed up what we stole and then went to the bathroom.

"Y'all look really silly sitting in that bathtub without the water in it," Dante said as he reached down and put the stopper in the tub. He took a little dab of bubble bath and let one droplet hit the bottom of the tub. We took our dicks back out. We started peeing. We peed in the tub and in their store-bought hair. It was brown liquor piss, too. We had been holding it on purpose since we left the Rooftop. We knew what those bitches was plotting when we saw them earlier in the day at Willie Burgers. Hood muthafuckas may move a little different in other parts of the country but the game stays the same and we recognized it. We pissed enough between the four of us for them to soak in it until their folks came. I felt for the one at the bottom a little bit cuz she had to soak in the piss the most. But it was Bridgette, the one that made the call to her crew so it was justified.

We hit the block laughing like a muthafucka. Doing little shit like that was still fun to us. The deeper we got into this life, it became less humorous and very serious. We had to enjoy it even if it was young adolescent shit cuz it was probably the last time we were going to have some dumb fun as a group. Shannon flipped his bipolar switch and went from laughing to being mad.

"Selfish ass muthafuckas."

"Here he goes. What could you possibly be mad at now?" I had to ask.

"We taped them bitches mouth up before I got to get my dick sucked. Y'all only think about yourselves."

"Nigga what?"

CHAPTER 14

IT FELT GOOD BEING back in LA. I had major business to take care of. My plate was full. First thing I was going to do was move into my own crib. My lady hipped me to these luxury apartment units called the Park LaBrea near the Tar Pits. I would still be in the hood; I'd just be watching it from the outer perimeter. Chips definitely inspired me to spend a little bit of money on my fly spot. I was a couple of months away from turning 19 but I wasn't about to live like a kid in a joint that looked like a college dorm. I was thinking of flying Chips out to Los Angeles and letting him put his expert touch on it but I was too eager to wait. I knew it would be at least a week before he was able to travel. It was also that new gear I bought from Bergdorf's and Bloomingdale's in New York triggering my impatience. I wanted to put it on in my new crib, stand in the mirror, and really get that feeling like *I have arrived*. I wanted to get all my personal shit out of the way before we hit that Hustler Crew out of Palms. We wanted to put a hurtin' on them. Those were some arrogant and disrespectful little bastards. We got word they were talking real sideways since we went on that trip. Predictable muthafuckas, they did just what we expected. They took us for being weak. They have been calling us every kind of bitch and fag for the past week like they truly forgot what our original gender really was. They thought we had small balls or none at all. We took offense to that, but we are known for our defense; we hit back.

I stopped by my mama's house first; I like the way that sounded. It came out so natural. I needed to grab a couple of thousand out of my safe to put a deposit on *My Crib*! After that, I was going to get my car detailed, hit a mall to buy my mama something nice, and take her out to dinner in Beverly Hills. We were going to celebrate my independence and retire her *as long as you're living under my roof* house rules.

I walked up the stairs. I had my head looking down as I searched for my keys. I looked up and the front door was slightly open. Mama was still supposed to be out of town so this was not a good look. All my pistols were stashed in my room, too. I eased the door open and slipped in. I went to the kitchen and got one of Mama's Ginsu Knives and thinking that muthafucka better slice meat like it said on the brochure. I eased back to my room.

The door was broke and knocked off the hinges. "DAMMIT!" My safe was the only thing missing and everything that was inside. All of my guns except the one that jams, my passport, some valuable intel that I had on a couple of joints we were going to rob, and naked pictures of my freaky females. I checked my mama's room and her television was missing and her dresser drawers were open and her undergarments were shuffled around but nothing was taken from what I could see.

It didn't make sense. It wasn't a rival crew out there foolish enough to run up in Mama's apartment. I never underestimate anyone in this life but I don't think these little young niggas developed heart like that in a week. They needed a lot of time and tools to get that safe outta there. I had it bolted down with big construction screws. I had it so secured that when I moved to my new pad, the safe was staying at Mama's 'cause it was going to be too much work to deal with. They fucked the floor up something awful, too. The harsh reality I was facing was it was somebody I knew. I knew shit like this came with the life but I was damn sure trying to avoid it. I immediately started counting off the people that knew what I had in my room… on one hand. I never made it to the fifth finger. I was tapped. I needed that paper back. I had to call Shannon. I was holding 25 grand for him for sure, but I wasn't sure how much he put in the safe before we skipped town. "FUCK! Why is this Bullshit happening today! DAMN!"

$ $ $ $ $

Shannon entered his apartment. Khan was standing in the kitchen eating a bowl of Honeycomb cereal. He had the open box and carton of milk on standby when he was ready to refill his bowl.

"I hope you just as hungry for my money. Where's my money that you fucked off?" Shannon barked, never thinking of saying *Hello* at all.

"Damn, Shannon, I'm your brother. Can you say, what's up or something first before you come in here trippin' on a nigga?'"

"I'm not trying to hear all that shit! I ain't listening. Where's my money? We'll talk later. What you got? You better have something."

"Or what? You gonna do something? You ain't gon' do shit! I got your little funky forty G's. You need to check yourself. Mama always said you were a selfish bastard," Khan stated boldly 'cause he was in the clear to talk shit back.

"I ain't listening to you or Mama's bullshit. Y'all cost me ninety grand last year fucking it off. I'm trying to get y'all straight and set you up right so I can handle my business and y'all still be beggin'. Now where's my money?" Shannon bitched as he looked all around the house for his bread.

"It's in your room in the closet, asshole, " Khan said with a mouthful of cereal as he started reading the cartoons on the back of the Honeycomb box.

Shannon found the bag and kept bitching.

"You just left the money out in the open like this? What the fuck is wrong with you? Anybody could have come up in here and laid you down for this. What are you thinking?"

"Shut up, nigga! I just got here an hour ago, asshole. Stop talking to me right now 'cause you're upsetting my stomach. I want to enjoy my breakfast."

Shannon counted the money and yelled, "Fuck your breakfast! Throw that shit away and let's go down to CJ's Café and get some French Toast and Pancakes up in this bitch. Let's roll!" Shannon flipped his switch, as he often did. The phone rang. It was me calling him.

"Hello!"

"Hey Shannon…" He cut me off before I could give him the bad news.

"What up, Trav? Meet us at CJ's on Pico. We're about to get our grub on. We're leaving now. C'mon!"

"Whoa, man, we got a problem. The safe got hit while we was gone."

"What the fuck you mean the safe got hit? I don't want to hear no bullshit! Did they get my money and my new Uzi?"

"No muthafucka, they stole my shit and left yours with a note stuck to it, selfish ass nigga, I see what your brother be talking about now. But fuck all that, all our shit is gone. Who you been running your mouth to?"

"Nigga, don't be trying to flip shit around and don't fuck with me, Trav! It don't even sound right. Ain't nobody going to run up in your mama's house and break in that safe. It would take too much time."

"They didn't break in it. They took the whole safe out the floor!" I said, but I wouldn't believe my excuse if it were told to me so I didn't get mad at Shannon's reply.

"I really ain't going for that one. You had that shit bolted down too hard for the average street nigga to get making a simple house move. Hell no! You told somebody something! You better come up with that money, nigga!" Shannon screamed on me.

"Fool, you better check who you are talking to. I am not your little brother. I'll honor a head up squab any day if you ever want to throw these thangs. Now you best get focused on the big picture. We're in this together, muthafucka. *We* got hit hard. Let's put our ear to the streets and see who came up on a fortune out the blue."

"Fuck all that, Trav. Don't be trying to fuck me over! I'm on my way to your house right now and you better be there!" Shannon slammed the phone down in my ear. He stormed out of the bedroom and looked at Khan. He was still eating cereal and wiping the milk dripping down his chin with the back of his wrist.

Khan is only in the game because of his brother. He was down for the life but only when it was necessary. If Shannon were a mailman, Khan would have a lower pay job at the Post Office as well. Khan didn't have the hustle to come up on $40 grand even if it fell in his lap. Shannon knew that, but he didn't hesitate to ask.

"Hey, Khan," Shannon stood right in front of Khan. "Where did you come up on that paper that fast? You're not a Born Hustler and you too lazy to sell a product that sells itself, so what's up? Did you do some shit that I need to watch my back about? If you're involved, my name is automatically going to be attached to it. Talk to me."

"What you mean?" asked Khan as he set down his spoon and looked puzzled. "You told me to get focused and handle my business and stop fucking up. I'm seeing y'all coming up fast around here. That's why I didn't go on the trip. I felt ashamed that I didn't have the money I know I should be holding. Suge is rolling around here in new Corvettes and shit. Man, I'm trying to be down. Shit got dry on the streets for about three days so I stepped on that and took advantage of the situation. I hit a couple of rookies off that were desperate for some work. Nobody y'all do business with. Why you ask? What's with this third degree? Who was that on the phone?" It sounded good but it wasn't believable coming from Khan's track record of laziness.

Shannon played it off by telling Khan he was surprised by his Hustle. Shannon went back to his room. We always mark our money on the corner of the bills when we count it together. First we did it to keep track of what we counted. Then we realized that if we ever got hit we could always check that little mark or number on the bills. Shannon opened the bag Khan left for him. Shannon didn't want to open it. He didn't know how he was going to react if his brother paid him back with his own money. Shannon took a deep breath and unzipped the bag. He reached his hand inside and grabbed one of the ten thousand stacks bundled in a rubber band. Shannon was afraid to look. He closed his eyes and took a moment to think about it. Shannon took a long deep breath and held it in. He opened his eyes and looked at the money.

$ $ $ $ $

I called up north to tell my mama our crib had been invaded. They said she was already on her way back and should have been here by now. I looked at the phone strangely and hung it up. I called Suge. Not because I considered him a suspect, but to see if he saw anything odd on the streets.

"Hey what's up, Trav? I see you back in town. I hope you ready to cut down those Palm Tree niggas 'cause they have been real disrespectful on these streets putting too much shade on us and those little punk ass birds are shitting all over our cars," Suge spoke in code. He could have done a better job. Any rookie cop could dissect we need to cut those Palm Niggas down 'cause they been shitting on our name.

"I want to holla at you about something. What are you doing?" I asked.

"I'm going to come through. I want you to see this new Corvette I just bought a couple of days ago, I got these bitches bringing... wait, hold up Trav, my other line is ringing, hold on," Suge clicked over to the other line.

I thought about what he said, *new Corvette.* My antennas immediately went up when he said. *How did he get Corvette money that quick and he just bought a Z Turbo and a Harley?* This money missin' got me trippin'. I know my nigga Suge wouldn't play me like that. We are playing for big stakes in this life now. Trust and loyalty truly get tested on the level we are reaching. Not Suge though… my mind was fucking with me. My mind is really fucking with me now 'cause Suge still hasn't clicked back over. Soon as I thought it: *click-click*.

"Man, this muthafucka Shannon is out of pocket again! He's calling here with Gangster threats saying his money is missing and I was the only one in town that knew where y'all's money was. Let me call you back before I have to seriously hurt this nigga. I know I ain't the gunman in the crew but I swear to God, Trav, if he pulls that shit on me like he tried to do to Dante over that scandalous bitch of his, I am going to hurt him. Talk to your boy, Trav. Talk to Your Boy! I'll hit you back!"

Shannon is checking Suge? And here we go.

Shannon always does shit on emotions and makes the situation worse than it is. And shit already be fucked up so imagine where Shannon takes us sometimes. Well, I hoped he checked his slow-ass money-counting brother, too, since he's going there. Those two were on my list with Khan higher than Suge. Like I said, I didn't think Suge stole it but I can see him getting caught slipping 'cause he doesn't stay with his gun on his hip, and then end up getting kidnapped by those Palm niggas and pistol-whipped until he gave up the spot. Since that wasn't the case it only left Khan, my Woman, and Shannon… 'cause he ran his mouth too fuckin' much. That was my Top 4 but everybody was starting to look like suspects. I just needed that money back before they started looking like food.

$ $ $ $

I had to buy another gun (buy another gun?)

I had to drop another homie (drop another homie)

I got to keep a gun on me (I got to keep a gun on me)

Keep real homies for life -real homies for life

– MC EIHT & BROTHA LYNCH HUNG

CHAPTER 15

"I'M DOWNSTAIRS."

"Cool." That's all I said and put the phone down. Suge came by to get me out of my funk and hopefully get me back on my feet. I was going to have to press him for some bread. I needed him to hold me down. Soon as I get downstairs, Shannon came flying up the street and slammed on his brakes in front of Suge' brand new ride. He missed hitting the front end by inches.

Suge jumped out of his car. "You playing yourself real close on all levels. I'm not in the mood for your shit today, Shannon. I told your fuckin' ass on the phone I didn't have nothing to do with your money." Shannon had his gun in his hand. He looked at me like I broke in my own house.

"Where did you get the money for this Vette? What the fuck is this, Trav? You about to roll with this nigga and buy yourself a Corvette, too?" Shannon stared hard at us like we were marks. I put my hand in my pocket, but pulling out an old .22 against a new .45 might get me shot on an accident from the nigga laughing at me.

"I am not in the mood for your shit, Shannon. Now if you want to get to the bottom of this shit, we about to roll to Suge's crib and put our ear to these streets. I need mines. So if you need yours, I highly suggest you follow us over there. Matter of fact, I'm gonna ride with you," I told Shannon straight up and opened the passenger door of his ride. Shannon opened his door real relaxed, like it was all-good. I snatched his gun out of his hand and yanked his muthafuckin' ass all the way in the car by his wrist.

Out of respect and friendship, I refused to point the gun directly at him. That wasn't a good look. But I put the barrel across the bridge of his nose and kept it pointed outside the window and I said, "Today is going to be the last day you ever have your gun out while you talking to the men that love you, fool. We are the ones that are going to war with you, bail your black ass out of jail, get the ransom money up when they kidnap your black ass, and take care of your family if God forbid something happens to you. I'm all in nigga, but I'm playing by the rules of this game. We have plans, remember? Stay focused, Shannon. I'm not telling you how to survive in this life—you have to do you—but know I'm just as crazy as your muthafuckin' ass if I need to be."

BOOM!

I let off a shot through the window. The bang was so loud it scared the shit out of me. My ears were ringing something awful. That was not a good idea, but it takes self-sacrifice dealing with a demon like Shannon. He has to know you are willing to do more than he's willing to do or equal for him to respect your gangster. I kept his gun and then walked over to Suge.

"Matter of fact, let me drive this fly muthafucka," I said and hopped in the driver's seat, adjusted the rearview, and whipped that Vette around on the street. Shannon followed us to Suge's crib. Every time I looked in the rearview mirror, Shannon was mad-dogging me with evil intentions on his mind. The vibe was fucked up between all of us. I was picking Suge's brain as we were driving. Suge has hustle but he came up too fast in a week.

When we got to his new crib, he put my theory to rest quick. Shannon was only fool enough to press the issue and played himself like a chump. Suge didn't even want to play him like chump change, but that Shannon has a way of bringing shit out of us in bad ways.

"Hey Suge, you still ain't told me where you got that money to get that car."

"How much did y'all lose like 50 grand or some small shit like that?" Suge asked and clapped his hand in the air twice. A fine ass foreign bitch wearing an elegant gown came in the living room with a bag of cash. "Fifty G, meet my friend Trav and that's Shannon. Trav, Shannon, meet Fifty Grand." Suge introduced us but he wasn't finished. He clapped his hands four times and another fine bitch from Germany or somewhere like that came out. He gave the same introduction and introduced her as 100k with a Capital K. She had a briefcase and opened it up on the coffee table. Suge raised his hands up again and paused in mid air, "Do I need to introduce you to the twins Quarter Mill and Half a Mill or do you see I don't need your little funky fifty grand. Now respect what we got in the game or get the fuck out my house!"

"Damn Suge, what you been into, man?" I asked as I looked past the money and into his eyes.

"Shit, it ain't nothing but a hustle. Just testing some shit out, you know. So what you need to hold, Trav, to get you back on your feet? I'm kind of pressed for time."

"That 50 Bag would fit me just nice."

"C'mon man! I'll let you hold ten grand. Y'all were in New York too long around cats that get down like that. This is LA. When we learn how to build that trust among each other like we should, then holding a million dollars wouldn't be second-guessed, but this nigga Shannon is pressing me like I robbed you. And you didn't accuse me, Trav, like this disrespectful nigga here but I felt your energy in the car and that shit hurt me a lot. But I understand why and the way we was raised in this game to be independent stiffens our unity. The shit we are trying to pull off is a learned practice. We were not taught the game correctly by the OGs in these LA streets. Let's get this shit together first or leave it alone!"

CHAPTER 18

There's a right and a wrong way
to love somebody...

MY MOOD WAS ALL fucked up and distorted. I went by Toni's house later on that night. I went over there looking to get into a fight. If it's true about taking frustrations out on the one closest to you, Toni was about to get hit with an avalanche of my bullshit. My shit was falling apart and coming down hard. Toni opened the door with the biggest smile on her face. She was so happy to see me after my little trip. She had the debut album by this new dude named Keith Sweat on in the background. All the girls were going crazy over that album. I've watched young girls start crying while they played that album. Toni had the candles lit. The weed was rolled already and the drink was on the table. She attempted to leap in my arms but I put the brakes on her in mid-flight. I caught her and put her feet back to the floor.

"Where did you get the money to get that expensive diamond necklace I've never seen that before?" I immediately asked when I saw her neck shining.

"When did my man become an average jealous nigga? I've never seen that before," Toni answered my question with a question and pissed me off even more.

"Don't play with me, dammit. I don't give a fuck about some fool tricking off his money on a necklace. I asked you where you got the money from. And this is the last fucking time I'm going to ask you nicely."

"You didn't ask me nicely the first time. What is this shit all about, Trav? It's a lot of things I have you've never seen before. What are you getting at?"

I looked around her pad for anything else suspicious. I loved Toni but she is cut from that cloth. She's down for the hood. Her pops is in the game. She knows how to maneuver in these streets. She could be capable of anything.

"Hey look, my fucking spot got hit and they got me for everything."

"I'm really hoping you don't think I have something to do with that Trav."

"I'm not accusing you, but I'm not thinking you didn't have nothing to do with it either. Everybody is guilty right now."

"Everybody, huh? Even your own mama?"

"You damn right! My grandmamma, too!" I lied but was pissed when I said it.

"Don't you let this game fuck you up, Trav. I know we ain't been together long but I'm with you. I want you to tell me, 'Baby we got hit' and *we* do what *we* have to do from there," Toni said with the emphasis on *We*. I felt like Shannon. I wasn't listening.

"That sounds sweet and whatever the fuck you are trying to make it sound like, but you still ain't told me where the fuck you got those diamonds! All that side stepping and ducking of my question contradicts all that shit you just said. All that loyalty in the game doesn't mean shit to me right now. I need you to be straight up," I demanded. Toni chose to push my buttons on purpose instead of answering the damn question.

"If I didn't do anything to you to get them, why does it matter?"

"Bitch, 'cuz my money is missing and you have about half of that mysteriously around your neck and if you don't answer my muthafuckin' question both of my hands are going to be around your neck choking the fuck out of you!" I yelled and meant everything I said. Toni decided to test me to see if I was the type of nigga that does what he says. It was something she needed to see in me as well.

"Fuck you Trav. I ain't telling you shit. You don't see nothing about me that resembles a bitch, but I do have a cold-hearted bitch in me and you about to bring it out. So check yourself in my house, nigga! I don't know who the fuck you think I AM!"

"Bitch!" I grabbed Toni around her throat and lifted her off her feet. Toni swung with her free hand and slapped me upside the head. She tried to catch my face but I saw it coming. She swung again, but I didn't feel it. I slammed her back against the wall and the cheap plaster cracked under pressure. We left a hole in the wall shaped like her ass print. I dropped her to her feet. She looked at me dead in the eye like she wanted to kill me.

"My favorite Aunt left me these diamonds when she died. I only wear them on serious occasions. I thought my man coming home was one of those times. Fuck You, Trav!"

Damn. So Toni checked me and made me feel foolish. I took a deep breath. Soon as the air left me, she slapped me hard across the face. She caught me good. I never hit a woman in my life but I reacted like a person that just got the dog shit slapped out of him. I slapped her back. She dug her nails in my chest and ripped the whole front of my shirt off. I grabbed her wrist and pulled her close to my chest. She broke loose from my grip and started tongue kissing me and taking my belt off. We were kissing and ripping off each other's clothes. We were naked in seconds. She jumped up on me and wrapped her thighs around my waist. I said, "This some freak shit!"

"I know, baby… feed my demon!"

I lifted her ass up and spread her cheeks open. I inserted my Sweet Cock deep into her pussy. It was so wet I could feel the juices traveling down my shaft. I started stroking those walls with nice long strong strokes. Toni arched her back so I could get all of it. She raised back and positioned herself so she could see the wetness she was coating my dick with. *"How Deep is Your Love"* came on and Toni expressed all her deepest desires and fantasies.

We hopped across the room with Toni still straddled on my Shaft.

I hit the back of the pussy every time I landed on both feet. Her pussy was spasming every single hop until we made it to the other side of the room. I put her back against the wall and started digging that pussy out so good. It was extremely wet so my strokes were killing that spot. I was digging that pussy out. Then I started banging it out. The screams of passion Toni let out made my dick grow bigger and harder and thicker. I was trying to knock the bottom out that muthafucka! Toni bit me hard on my shoulder and broke the skin. I could feel her vagina walls collapsing and convulsing on my hard thickness. We touched every wall in that house. Toni dug her nails in my back and I exploded hot semen up in her like a volcano. She went limp and I felt flush. I carried her to the bedroom on shaky legs. I laid her down on the soft bed real easy and laid down next to her. She found her spot on the left side of my chest, snuggled against it, and got cozy. We were both knocked out sleep in less than a minute.

"How deep is your love…"

CHAPTER 17

TENSIONS BETWEEN US LOCS were getting thick. We had a grip of money missing and no clues. A week had gone by and nothing. We needed answers. It was so much money on the streets at this time everybody had new materialistic items so shaking all of them down to find information would take us years. My Top Suspects all checked out and had nothing to do with it.

Shannon was still confused on his end as well. That money Khan gave him wasn't ours. It was a relief from that perspective. Shannon still wanted to know how he got it but once he had it in his hands he seemed to care less where it came from. It was no longer his concern. I would hate to see what might have happened if it really were Khan. Shannon has some serious character issues. I was really curious to see how that would have played out.

But there was no time to waste thoughts on unattainable bullshit. We were turning up the pressure on the streets in the ugliest ways possible. We made threats to every gang we didn't like. All that did for us was create enemies as well as expose some new enemies we never had or thought we didn't have up until that point. But even after all that, we still didn't have that money back. It was crazy because the streets would have been started talking by now even if it was some made up he said-she said bullshit. Only word on the streets was The Westside Gangsters were coming down hard, pressing crews for information with guns out and being very aggressive and disrespectful about it. *"Watch your back, these niggas is trippin'."*

It was true. We are not going to deny that. We were trippin'! We burned a few bridges that week, but fuck it, it can't be repaired now. Shannon and I's relationship was getting no better. Our quest to find our money was the only common interest we shared now. We looked at each other sideways blaming the other one for getting robbed. Of course, it was all on me 'cuz it was at my house. Now all that going back and forth was coming to a head.

We all met up in the back parking lot of the Original Roscoe's Chicken and Waffles on Washington near LaBrea. It was a lot of old dudes that looked like Blues Players that frequented the joint. The front of Roscoe's was a bar with an old jukebox that kept songs cranking on it. It had a little dance floor but it looked nothing like a club. The back of the joint was where you got your food. Our parents went there a lot and to the Parisian Room up the block. It was a good meeting spot on neutral grounds. Khan and Shannon came together. I rode with Suge; Dante came with Soncho. Dez didn't show up. He has some business he needed to tend to. Soncho said he got word that somebody from HKK heard that those fools we laid down from the Number Blocks was coming back on us. At this point, we were not in a position to hear any more speculation stories. I personally removed the head of that number block crew so the rest of them were useless.

Shannon and I locked eyes and mad dogged each other soon as he pulled up. He got out of the car like something was on his mind.

"Don't walk toward me acting like you want to do something. I'm tired of you huffing up every time we see each other. What the fuck you wanna do?" I said and initiated the conflict. He couldn't back down now and I didn't expect him to.

"Well, what you want to do then, nigga?" Shannon said as he took his pager off his hip and tossed it to his brother. Khan was walking up, but I knew he would let us catch a fair one. He was going to make sure it didn't get too vicious. We squared up and were damn near nose-to-nose. I could smell the acid on his breath coming from the pit of his stomach. We were both known to throw the first punch in a fight but neither of us flinched. I know we were both thinking *swing first* out of habit, but something was intervening. I can't say it was love because at that point all that childhood sandbox shit, spending the night at each other's house, and riding skateboards together didn't mean shit to us. We were ready to squab. His jaw was calling me. I clinched my fist ready to answer it.

Two I-Rocs, a BMW, and a Benz 190 rolled up in the parking lot. Khan peeped game and said, "Hey you fools! Chill the fuck out. These Shady Palm Tree niggas is rolling up."

Now we were really out of bounds, beefing with each other and these fools roll up on us and we didn't have one strap between us handy. Damn! We wouldn't have made it to our stash boxes in our rides if we tried. They caught us slippin'.

"Look at this punk ass shit. These bitch ass niggas are having a lovers' quarrel. As close as you're standing to each other, you might as well just kiss and make up," said this fool named Kenyan who just promoted himself as the spokesman or leader of the crew. We saw him as the first one we were going to knockout for running his mouth in a disrespectful way. Tensions were too thick between Shannon and I to get into character and play the con on these fools. We were supposed to be pretending like they ran us out of town. But seeing Shannon and I on the verge of fighting actually played in our favor.

They saw real weakness in us now. Kenyan spoke on it. "I haven't seen you busters around in a minute. They said Westside Gangsters were tough. They were wrong. Westside is pussy. You're not even a gang anymore. We took your hood without a gun. We heard you got niggas running up in your mama's house robbing you and shit. What the fuck you still doing living with your mama anyway? Now look at you… you look pitiful. I heard they are hiring down at the Post Office. This game ain't for y'all. So what you doing, y'all working here now at Roscoe's? Well if you faggots are finished kissing, why don't you get back to work and get us some Chicken and Waffles plates out in this bitch?"

I tried to keep cool and play the con but Shannon didn't stay in character.

"You know something about my money, muthafucka. You better tell me something!"

"Or what, Pussy? I didn't take your money but I wish it were me that did it. I was going to rob you eventually but somebody else moved on it first. But trust me, we are looking for whoever hit you 'cuz that was OUR money! So let us handle that. Now take your asses back to the kitchen and get our food," Kenyan rebutted with extreme confidence. We knew by the way Kenyan was talking he already had his hand on his gun. The longer he talked shit, the more he was really starting to believe his own hype.

The rest of his crew was getting cocky, too. The short one with the wide mouth that had the big teeth that always showed up named Bullet or Bullet Ze' walked up on Khan like he wanted his watch. "This is our hood now. Just standing here is taxable by law. I think you need to come up off that watch, homie. That's mine now."

Khan knew he could whip homeboy with the gun in his hand. There is no worse feeling than getting punked by a punk. Khan came up off his watch but it came with a look that let homie know he was coming back for it with interest. We started easing back to our cars before they all started getting ideas.

"Y'all got that, homies. We don't want no problems with y'all right now but we'll meet up again," I said, hoping I didn't overdo it. They knew I wasn't bitch-made so I couldn't act scared or they would have detected it was a set up. We retreated but still gave them the impression we wasn't quite yet defeated. We made it to our cars and stabbed out.

"We should have killed those niggas," Man-Man said. He was one of the shooters in their crew.

"They don't want to see us in these streets, besides our parents eat here. You're trying to make their spot hot. Fuck those pussies man. They're done. Let's go get that Scoes Special. I'm hungry as a muthafucka," Kenyan concluded and proceeded inside to fill his belly.

$ $ $ $ $

Suge dropped me back off at my mama's apartment. I had everything in my room packed up ready to move. I didn't want to spend the bread Suge loaned me until I started generating more dollars. I don't like spending money when I don't have it rolling in. I hate it even more when I don't have it to spend. I'm used to living a certain way and I can't go back now.

I was heading up to the apartment and forgot that I left a phone number I had written down on a piece of paper in my glove compartment. I met this Belizean girl named Desiree that said she had pounds of some good weed for cheap. That was the type of weed we would take out of town to those dry areas and make a killing off dime bags. We would never pay those prices for that quality of marijuana. It was all profit, too. We only smoked it if we ran out of our own personal and that was only twice.

Anyway, I had parked about a half a block up the street. As I was walking up to my ride to get that number, my pager went off. I looked at the number and it was triple sixes. I was like, "What the Fuck? I don't play that shit!" I was so mad I gripped my pistol. I knew it was Shannon playing his sick games, but he went too far this time. I stopped in mid stride and did an about face to call that fool and let him know I was on my way to put hands on him. I looked to my left and saw one of those little Palm Tree niggas creeping down low from behind one of the neighbor's cars. I busted on his ass but I missed him on purpose. I didn't want to drop a body on my mama's block. Instead I blew the taillight of the car out and caused the broken glass to shatter in his face. He immediately grabbed at his face and started shooting blindly. Car alarms started going off all down the block. His getaway car pulled up and ushered him in the car. I rose up and licked off two shots as they were stabbing out. I busted out the side and back window. I checked my body and then I checked my ride. He put a nice ugly 32-caliber bullet hole in my trunk. I was pissed the fuck off now.

I headed upstairs and my mama was so mellow she didn't even hear those shots. I was glad because I was not in the mood to explain. I saw Mama went shopping above her means but I didn't even question it. I had run out of suspects a week ago. I was finally starting to chalk it up as a loss. "What up, Mama? Why you doing all this shopping and it's not Christmas time?" I asked.

"Ladies need to treat themselves to nice things sometimes. Why are you worried about it? I'm paying for it. I won the monthly $1,000 raffle at work and went shopping," Mama answered.

"I'm not worried. I have enough things to worry about in my life. I don't need any extra. Are you going out tonight or something?" I said.

"Yes, I am, *father*. I'm going out with Shannon's mama tonight. What's going on with you two?"

"Just hood shit that comes with the game. That's all," I answered like it was no big deal.

"I hope you guys don't let this stuff you do come between you. We are like Family. His mama and I are best friends. You and Shannon have been best friends almost your whole life. You guys need to put your differences aside and make up," Mama stated like she was supposed to.

I didn't want to hear a speech. Nothing sounds right when my money is funny. "I got you, Mama. Be safe out there tonight. I'll see you tomorrow."

"Where are you staying tonight?" Mama asked being nosey.

"I don't know yet, probably with Toni. I'll let you know."

"You still live here officially so don't play with me Trav!"

I looked at mama and just smiled. That was all I could do to avoid her drama.

CHAPTER 18

"HEY DANTE!"

"Who's that?"

Pop! Pop! Pop! Pop!

"This is P Town, nigga!

Dante dove in the street between a car and the curb to take cover. The car burned rubber and peeled off. Dante heard the shooter laughing off in the distance. Dante got up off the ground pissed. He was wearing all white and some Stan Smith tennis shoes fresh out the box.

"Ain't this about a bitch! These little niggas are starting to get on my muthafuckin' nerves!"

$ $ $ $ $

Soncho was at the Mobil gas station on Cadillac and LaCienga in PBG Hood.

"Hey, didn't you use to go to Pasteur Jr. High back in the day? US History, seventh grade? You Soncho; right?"

"Yeah I did, but I don't think you know me, homie. Step!" Soncho warned the strange dude that questioned him and for good measure, Soncho pressed his gun hard in dude's chest just in case he didn't hear him. The dude peed on himself a little bit.

"Damn brutha! I didn't like US History either but you must have really hated it. Shit, my bad!"

Even when Soncho realized he made a mistake, he didn't apologize to homie for being cautious. The green light was on us. Those little Palm Boys was running muck. They spray painted P Town and P-City all through our hood. They were riding through yelling *Westside Pussy!* Our little homies would throw up the set but they were no threat to those bitch ass niggas. All it did was get them beat up and jacked.

Since we were having internal problems, it was making us look weak on the streets. We were supposed to smash them weeks ago. This wasn't a good look. Dez had his hand in something so he missed a lot of our bickering, but we already knew he wasn't too happy from what he was hearing. And he definitely sent word back to get our shit together and handle that business. He wanted to cut those Palm Tree niggas down before they started growing. He knew they were going to be a problem 'cause they had something to prove. They were arrogant and they came from a little money. That meant they were in it for the rush. That addiction is dangerous. They were applying a lot of pressure and we weren't doing anything to stop it. It got bad.

$$\$ \ \$ \ \$ \ \$ \ \$$

Shannon and I hadn't spoken or made eye contact in over a month. It could have been longer. I wasn't really keeping track. We both had spots out of town so we tended to our own business. Our mothers were the only link between us. The homies just chilled with us separately. They didn't talk about what the other one was doing too much.

I was finally in my own crib. My pad was on the second floor. I flew Chips out to interior decorate. I thought I would enjoy his company, but he spent the entire three days he was out here lecturing me on the value of friendship and loyalty in the game. I appreciated his words of wisdom and his company but it was *all day*. He was relentless with it.

"Call your man! Fix this shit, son! Call your man! Call your man right now! You need each other in this shit we in, son! I saw it in his eyes. He wouldn't hesitate to peel a fool's wig back for you! And you the same for him, son! I don't fuck around with suckers! You need each other! Call your Man! Get him on the phone and get that money wit your man. You at War right now, Son! At war, man! Your Soldiers aren't unified. That's means you're divided, and separation ultimately leads to disintegration! Call your man on the Phone. Get him on the Phone; Chips want to talk to him too. Call your man..." As much as I wanted to just so Chips could give me a break, it didn't go down. Needless to say, Son was extremely disappointed.

$ $ $ $ $

The Thanksgiving Day Dinner came around and I had no choice but to see Shannon, but I was definitely going to make it brief. The festivities were going to be at Shannon's parents' apartment. I promised my mama I would come but I didn't want to eat there. All Shannon's family ate was pork, from the Rooter to the Tooter. They were having Pig, Hog, Lard Coated Yams, Pork & Greens, Mac & Fatback, Swine Potato Pie for dessert, and a lot of liquor to drink. Since I moved out, I hadn't had any swine. I wasn't turning Muslim or Jewish or no shit like that; I just no longer had a taste for it. Toni didn't cook it either. Her father didn't dig on the swine, as Toni put it. I was going to have steak, lobster, salmon, and vegetables at her mom's house.

"You two really make a cute couple. He sure is handsome, Toni, just like your father," Toni's mother said as they led me in their nice modest house in the Crescent Heights District.

"Thank you Mrs. Williamson. It is a pleasure to see you again. I brought you a Bean Pie and a Sweet Potato Pie and these flowers. Do you have a vase I can put them in?"

"Oh Trav! You're so nice. Toni, he's a keeper. How did you know we liked Bean Pie? Did Toni tell you that?"

"Yes, she did, ma'am. She said it was her father's favorite."

"It sure is. He'll be home soon. Did Toni tell you?"

"Yes, ma'am. I'm looking forward to meeting him but I know he's even more excited to be coming home," I said but I was thinking, *Pops is going to be killing that old cock when he gets home.* Toni's mama was still fine. If it were any of my past girlfriends' mothers, I would have swapped them for sure, but Toni was special. I am not going to lie; I needed her. I looked at Mrs. Williamson's ass when she walked away. I said, "Mrs. Williamson, if it's true I can determine how Toni is going to look in the future by seeing her Mother, then I'm going to be in heaven. You are breathtaking Mrs. Williamson."

"How many times have I got to tell you to call me Tanya?" Mrs. Williamson teased me in a seductive voice as she struck a pose and threw her head back. All the relatives seating around the room all started laughing. Toni punched me hard in the stomach with the side of her fist.

"What? I just gave your Mother a compliment!" I said, trying to play it off. I knew I was busted.

"You a damn lie; you were staring at my Mother's butt a little too long. That's sick!" Toni said and rolled her eyes.

"Sick to whom? Those cakes will bring a dead man back to life," I spoke the first thing that came to my mind but I didn't mean for it to come out like that.

Toni kept playfully hitting me and then introduced me to everybody in the house. I met both sides of the family and a few close friends of theirs. Toni whispered in my ear and pointed out a relative's friend of a friend that came along for Thanksgiving dinner that I did find very interesting. There was something about her that I liked a whole lot. We were definitely going to get acquainted sooner than later so I didn't even bother introducing myself to her at that time. Toni didn't press the issue either. But she was pressing up against me to arouse me so we could slip to the bathroom for a quickie.

I was having a good time with Toni's family and friends. The meal was delicious. I lost all track of time. A little after 8pm, my pager started going off like crazy. It was Shannon's parent's number with 911 after it three times. I knew it was my mama looking for me. If I hadn't promised her already, I wouldn't be going over there. I didn't answer the page at first. When she paged me twice more I had to call because everybody in the house was starting to look at me like I was a street pharmacist. I played it off. "This is my Mom, you guys know how that is. Her only son is not there for Thanksgiving dinner 'cause he's with another woman. I can feel the tension through my Motorola."

I finally called the number back and Khan answered. It was loud in the background. I could hear his crazy ass pops just as loud and drunk as can be. I must admit I did miss that. Their pops is hilarious when he's drunk.

"What up Khan. Long time no see. My mama just paged me. Where she at?"

"She's in there. You coming through?"

"Yeah, I promised her I would shoot through." I stated like I was depressed about it.

"That's the only reason you're coming? You don't want to see the homies? You all hugged up with Toni. Bring her through," Khan said in a drunken state of mind.

"All right. But where's my mama?"

"She's in there just come man... wait, ...what? This is your son on the phone now..." I heard some voices in the background. "Your mama said hurry up. Come on!" Khan hung up the phone. It was going to be one of those nights. I had to get some liquor in me before I got there. Being sober in a room full of loud drunk emotional people is not fun at all. On the way over there I stopped at the store, copped me a 40 of Old E and took that bad boy to the head.

$ $ $ $ $

When I pulled up on the street I could already hear "*Bad Mama Jamma*" coming from the apartment. I walked upstairs. I didn't have to knock because the door was wide open. Even with air circulating, the living room was still full of thick cigarette smoke. The ashtray was overflowing with cigarette butts still burning. Shannon's pops and his friends were so drunk all they could do was chain smoke and talk shit. Soon as I walked in, I knew my colorful baby blue Polo shirt would catch Pops' eye.

"There he is! C'mon in here boy! What you got in that bag?"

"Your favorite. Beefeater Gin. You know I had to come right."

"And you came right on time, too. I love you like my own son. Y'all still dress like a faggot, but you all right with me. You want a drink? It's some pig in there, too. You hungry?

"Hey, Shauntez," that was Pops' real name. His buddy Ted from work interrupted him.

"What, nigga? I'm talking to my other son."

"I don't think you should be using words like nigga and faggot around the kids. It's offensive."

"And who the fuck are you, nigga? The faggot expert? This is my house, muthafucka! I say what the fuck I want to say. I love Trav. I love Trav just like he's my own. Don't I, Trav? Don't I? I've been drinking, but we talking man shit right now. This muthafucka over here is trying to be a gay liberator! What the fuck is wrong with that nigga here? Cockeyed muthafucka. Do you know they made this nigga here supervisor at work? He don't do shit, he just laughs every time the white folks laugh. He doesn't even know they trickin' is dumb ass.... What's that fragrance you got on, boy? You smell good like Honey Blossoms in the spring. You need to talk to my two sons, they come in here smelling like a pair of testicles sometimes...." Pops continued his rant non-stop. "Look at that big bitch going back to the kitchen for another plate. Damn! She's already 400 pounds. Any of y'all ever see her big ass naked? You can't see no pussy! That's how much belly she got, it's just a bunch of meat across here!" Pops said as he used his hands trying to be descriptive.

I moved over to the dining room to where all the women were sitting. They were just as tipsy as the men. A couple of them were getting too friendly when I gave them hugs. My mama and Shannon's mama were talking over each other as they were both trying to tell the same story at the same time. I wasn't even in the house good before they were trying to send me back out to the store.

"Where is the stuff we asked for from the store?" My mama asked me. I didn't have a clue what she was talking about.

"You didn't ask for anything. I was just at the store. I took care of Pops," I explained.

"So you can bring Shauntez something, but not your Mother... see what I'm talking about, girl? He only thinks about his own ass!" Mama stated as she started talking shit about me to her friends. Shannon's mama had to add her ad-libs.

"Ain't none of them shit! We did all we could to raise them and they won't even offer to bring you a piece of penny candy from the damn liquor store. That's a damn shame. Oh, ungrateful bastards. Where is my good for nothing son? Shannon! Shannon! Get out here! We need you and Trav to make a run to the store!"

The air of irritation left my body. If I were two years younger, I probably would have pouted. I did not sign up for all this extra shit. Shannon came out of the room bitchin'. We didn't acknowledge each other or make eye contact. There wasn't even any negative tension. We were invisible to each other. Shannon's mama said, "You guys still mad at each other? You guys are so silly and stubborn like bulls... just like your fathers." Pops heard that as he was walking to the restroom.

"I heard that shit! Ain't that about a Bitch! Stubborn? Woman, I'll deal with you when I come out of the toilet...Damn!! Who just pissed in here? You need some water in your gotdamn system. It smells like ammonia in this muthafucka!"

My mother was feeling herself since she got a little raise at work. I was happy 'cause she wasn't in my pockets as much. She still hit me up for cash if she was strapped for it, but not like before. She reached way down in her bra and came out with 40 bucks. "Bring us some more brandy for the eggnog and some of that nasty shit Ted likes to drink, Old Granddad. Here's some money. I'll pay for it myself. I already know asking you to pay for it is going to be like pulling a tooth. Ol' cheap ass nigga! And he's going to take the money, too, you see this girl? … And bring back my change!"

"Shannon, get your mama the big bottle of rum, a two liter of Coca Cola, and some orange juice for your dad." Shannon stood there after his mama finished with her order and held his hand out for the money. His moms was pissed.

"See what I'm saying? He keeps all that money and all those damn guns here. If the police come while he's gone, they are taking my black ass to jail and I have to give him twenty dollars of my own money for a drink. I know I didn't raise you to be like this. Just like yo' daddy!" She reached down in her brassiere and gave Shannon twenty bucks. She said, "If it's more than that, you cover the rest. I know you got money, Shannon!"

"I ain't got it. I'm broke. Stop telling people what I bring over here. You don't know who could be listening," Shannon schooled his mom.

"Ain't nobody coming in here with that damn armory you got in there! Ain't nobody in here that crazy Shannon but you."

Pops came out of bathroom looking like he was ready for bed. "Damn. Y'all still ain't left for the store yet? Hurry the fuck up, I'm gon' be sleep in a minute. Are you niggas still mad at each other?"

We didn't answer Pops. He spoke for us like we knew he would.

"Listen. I can't tell you what to do 'cause you ugly muthafuckas is grown now. I love both of you like sons. I know we ain't blood, but we are Family. We're Family…. I done fucked around and forgot what

I was going to say... but you know what I meant to say... Shit, you probably fighting over some punk shit anyway."

"What's wrong? You couldn't find a hot pink gun to match your hot pink shirt?" Pops' friend Herbert chimed in. I don't know why he was laughing; his son is a sissy for real, washing some niggas draws in Pelican Bay right now. We paid him no mind. As we were walking out of the crib, Pops offered us more money but we didn't accept it.

"Are you sure you don't need no more money? Shit, everything is getting expensive nowadays. The cost of pussy even went up! Pussy used to cost about two dollars when I was a little boy, am I lyin', Ted? By the time I went to the Army, pussy went up to ten dollars and then I had to pay two dollars for the room. I said *sheeiiit, Bitch, let me pay you two dollars and keep this ten, and we can fuck outside!*"

$ $ $ $ $

Shannon and I left the apartment together to satisfy our parents since it was a holiday. We didn't say one word to each other. When we got downstairs, he went to his car and I went to mine. I must admit I did feel silly when we arrived at the liquor store the same time in separate cars.

Shannon got out of his car with his strap in his hand. I didn't take it as if it were for me because we were out of bounds now. *Technically,* it wasn't considered our hood anymore. It was P City. Palm Tree Killa is how I felt about that. I got out the car. My strap was in my pocket already so I didn't have to walk in the store like a cowboy going into a saloon.

There were two registers open. I walked straight to the counter. I ordered the 1.75 liter of Ernest and Julio Gallo and all the other shit. Shannon was in the back getting his pops some orange juice. He walked up to the counter as I was finishing my order. He placed his order. I searched my pockets for that wet forty my Moms gave me. I had about $3,000 on me but I kept that separate. Mama didn't lie on me. I wasn't going to buy her anymore liquor with my money. She was already passed her limit.

I felt her money in my back pocket kind of stuck to the lining. I unfolded the bills and got ready to hand them to the cashier, but then I noticed my marking in the corner of the bill. I pulled them back to take a closer look. It was the bills I had marked that were in my safe.

I didn't know what to feel. I didn't even realize what I was doing. I put one twenty back in my pocket and gave the cashier one. I still owed him another $18 and didn't even hear the cashier asking for it. I didn't feel betrayed as much as I felt embarrassed. I felt full fledge embarrassment.

I don't know why I did it at first, but I kind of glanced over at Shannon from the corner of my eye. He was already facing me, just staring. I turned to face him. Shannon had a tear in his eye. He reached his hand in his gun pocket and pulled out the $20 bill his mama gave him. It had his mark on the upper right corner of the currency. We just looked at each other. Shannon felt hurt, pain, and betrayal. I saw it all in his eyes. We didn't even speak on it. How were we supposed to react to that?

We just kept looking at each other with a different expression on our face each and every time that told what we were feeling. A lot of good OGs educated us about all the things that may come with being in this game we chose and we heard a lot of great information but not one, not even the elder gangster Pico Nikko out of Chicago, ever mentioned some shit like this would ever go down. Shannon and I have been through some major life threatening situations on our young journey but this ordeal here has generated the worst feeling ever. We both needed time to think.

CHAPTER 19

"IT'S LIKE CAN-DAAAY!"

I bent the corner with that 3-Wheel motion in my 1969 Chevy Impala. I was bumping that new shit "Candy" by Cameo. It was bangin' and I was boppin' my head and feeling myself something awful. I saw some of the homies from the other side and threw my set up. They threw their set up and smiled. They had to give it up to me. I was rollin' right. My paint job was too clean to hate on. The right song bumpin' at the right time definitely cures the savage beast. I was going west up Pico. Three cute broads caught my eye on the other side of the street. They were sashaying in front of Oki Dogs. I never understood why all my friends thought the food there was so good. I was the oddball out. It was overrated to me. They all acted like it tasted better than pussy or something. It was just a cheap ass hot dog wrapped in a tortilla. I hit a U-turn right in the middle of the street. I could already tell they liked something about me. They were cute but definitely hood related. The cute broads that liked hood shit on the Westside make their way around town but they don't come with drama that leads to a young death. They'll give their man's homies some pussy and rub them the wrong way but it doesn't get extremely violent.

I had seen these chicks around before. I wanted the chocolate brown skinned one with that soft natural Indian hair. Her jeans were tight and that fat ass looked right. I double-parked my ride on Pico and left the car door open. I left the sounds bumpin', too. Everybody was bobbing their heads to my music. I wasn't out of bounds, but we were at war. I had both of my 4-5's on me but I didn't have my eyes open. Tanya's pretty mouth had my undivided attention. I looked at her lips and into her mouth when she spoke instead of into her eyes. I'm so busy trying to spit some drag that I didn't even feel the eyes that were staring a hole in the back of my head. Tanya was semi-fucking around with one of the enemies from Palms named Pierre. I didn't know too much about him other than he was getting his money. He had a little player about himself but that's all I knew about him. However, Pierre knew more about me than I wish he had.

"There goes one of the Westside niggas slippin' right there. Damn his Low Rider is clean! I'm gonna hate to get blood on that interior. That muthafucka is cold!" said this little dusty buster they called Grim, not because he was a Reaper but because he looked like a gremlin. He was itching to earn some stripes.

"Which one is that?" Pierre asked.

"That's that fool, Trav Mack. He went to Fairfax. I didn't like him then," Grim answered impatiently. He was eager to peel my cap back.

"That's the cool one, too. I wish it were the fool Shannon. I don't like that muthafucka at all. He's a disrespectful sonovabitch!" Pierre shook his head. "Wait! Who is that he's talking to? I know that's not... is that fool trying to talk to my bitch? Is that Tanya?" Pierre asked suddenly. My back was facing them and it was kind of difficult to see Tanya from where they were sitting low in the car. Grim could barely see over the dashboard but he was going to be the instigator regardless.

"It damn sure is. Let's go lay his bitch ass down now."

"Naw-naw, let me quarterback this thing right. Tanya is a cute Westside bitch. She is not built for keeping her mouth closed after witnessing a daylight murder in front of Oki Dogs. Tanya is cute but she ain't got shit on Trav' broad Toni. Now that's a bad bitch. He's a fool to fuck that over. I need a down bitch like that on my team. I'll give that nigga ten Tanyas for half of a Toni... yes indeed, I got this.

Give this fool a pass today, homie," Pierre said.

"A pass? A pass? Are you crazy? This is one of the generals and a potential threat. He must be annihilated today! Fuck a Pass!" Grim yelled as he forgot his rank wasn't high enough to call shots in situations like that. Pierre tried to keep calm.

"Listen to me, man. Let me do this. This is my call."

"For a Bitch?" Grim asked in a way that rubbed Pierre wrong.

"Watch your tone! I told you I got this and leave it at that!"

"All right, but I got a bad gut feeling about this one. My instincts is telling me to drop this fool now 'cause I know if he were sitting in this same spot with the bead on us we would be dead already. He's not playing no games!"

He was right, too. I would have lit they ass up on sight. This is war. We were already past strategizing from the street perspective. I guess it was a good day because I would have never let me walk away.

I slid Tanya my card. She called me in less than an hour.

$ $ $ $

"Hey Khan, when was the last time Mama asked you for some money?" Shannon asked. He was definitely more pissed now than hurt since we discovered who hit our safe. I personally just shook my head and shrugged it off after awhile. It was a terrible lesson that we didn't want to have learned.

On our way back from New York, Shannon and I had already decided that part of the money we had stashed would be used to buy our parents their first homes they could actually own. So all they did was steal from themselves and ruin their future. They are still going to have to get that rent ready by the first of the month instead of just paying homeowner taxes once a year.

Shannon started treating his mama real evil. He was short with her or had no conversation for her at all. He still talked with Pops but he was unsure if Pops had a hand in it. We didn't think our mamas was that strong enough to move that safe alone, but shit, for 50-plus grand, ain't no telling what kind of miracles and great feats one can do once they put their mind to it.

"She hasn't asked me for nothing in a minute. I'm glad about that. Don't speak it into existence. I don't need that bill right now. I just got my paper up. Why you ask?" Khan wondered why his brother was worried about their mama and her naggin' for dollars.

"Well, she hasn't asked for nothing since we came back from New York. Was she acting strange while we were gone?"

"I don't remember. She was bitching as usual most of the time but nothing out of the ordinary. She did go shopping a couple of days before you got back but taking your money you leave around here for clothes ain't nothing new. What you thinking?" Khan asked again. He kind of felt where his brother was taking the conversation but Khan didn't want to hear it.

"I think Marlene and Mama were the ones that hit our safe," Shannon told a half-truth and confessed. He knew our mamas took that money but he said *I think* they were the ones. It was still the women that gave birth to us, and on that alone, we didn't want to say anything bad against them even if it were true. That shit is hard to do. We weren't neglected and abused as kids by our mothers. Drugs or any other ungodly habits did not plague them. This was crazy. This should not have happened like this.

Khan couldn't quite accept it either. The look on his face was blank. He put the blame on my mama just to try and make sense out of it. "I know Marlene was behind that shit. I knew she was scandalous. Mama wouldn't think of nothing like that by herself. I never trusted her when we were little. Remember when she used to hide us on the floor in the backseat of the car and sneak us in the drive-in theater? Marlene has always been sneaky like that," and with that, Khan had expressed how he really felt about my mama at that moment. The truth was he loved my mama far more than his. He said it on a few occasions so he was talking out of emotion on top of being hurt.

"I ain't apologizing, but I thought it was you at first. I still don't know where you got that money you owed me but it wasn't ours," Shannon told his brother with no shame about it.

"Fuck you Shannon. You just as scandalous as Mama and Marlene. How are you going to think I would do some shit like that?"

"You have a lazy hustle. You work when you want to but those moments are rare," Shannon admitted. It wasn't personal. It was the truth.

"Fuck you!" Khan paused. "So what happens next? Does she know that you know she stole the money?"

"Man, I don't want to talk about that shit with her. I'm never going to speak on it, but trust me, she's going to know that I know what the fuck she did," Khan spoke looking out into space. He bit down hard, clenched his teeth, and flexed his jaw muscles. Just thinking about it got his blood hot.

"Are you and Trav cool now? I hope so 'cause we need to lay those Palm fools down. They busted on me the other night at the 7-11 on Pico and Hi Point," Khan said as he shook his head.

As soon as Khan said that, Shannon forgot all about being mad at his mama. He did not like fools threatening to take his brother out. You were better off slapping his mama. He always felt that fools going after his brother were only doing that to get back at him. Khan was a Ryder, no question, but he didn't shoot first and ask questions later if he didn't have to. Shannon knew that. A lot of other Gangsters knew that, too. That's why Shannon always took it personal as well as a little guilt for his little brother following big brother in this life.

"What? They tried to kill my brother? Which one of those muthafuckas? Aww, it don't matter now anyway. They all done fucked up! Call Trav and let's get this work in! I'm tired of playing with these bitch ass niggas!"

$ $ $ $

"Hello?"

"Hey Marlene. How are you doing, girl?" asked Brenda, who was Shannon's mama.

"I'm okay, girl, but I really messed up my knee and back trying to move that heavy ass… you know. Is it cool to talk right now?"

Brenda put her hand over the phone and peeked back in the area of Khan's room then spoke, "I think Khan is in there with the door closed. Why? What's up?" Brenda asked.

"Do you think our sons know, you know, that we, you know, did that?" my mom asked, but too embarrassed to say what it was out loud. She was trying to make herself believe she didn't want to talk dirt over the phone, but that rule didn't apply at all. If the police did have the phone tapped, they would be thrilled knowing two more black families have been destroyed behind this genocidal plan they put in play.

"I'm not sure, but Shannon has really been acting funky toward me since Thanksgiving. He won't even talk to me and when he does his attitude has been real nasty. He's been treating me real fucked up, like shit! Why did you ask that? Is Trav acting funny?"

"He hasn't been treating me bad, but he hasn't said much since Thanksgiving either now that you mention it. The next day when he stopped by to pick up something, he said he found $20 in his room that the robbers must have dropped when they took the safe. He showed me the marks he left on the bill. I know that was one of the $20s I gave him that night. I checked the other money and, girl, I saw his marks on most of my bills. I didn't even notice it. Did you?" my mama asked.

"Hell, no, I didn't see shit. It still spends. What's on it?"

"Little numbers handwritten in the corner in pencil," Mama explained.

"I'm getting old, girl. I can't see that little shit written in pencil.

Shit, I can barely see my hand in front of my face," Brenda joked.

"Do you feel bad about what we did?" my mama asked, not as concerned as she was curious.

"At first I did, but the way Shannon's been acting lately, I don't feel shit now," Brenda stated trying to act tough but it was bothering her.

"Do you think our sons ever killed somebody before?" Mama's curiosity got the best of her again, but she was also worried like a mother should be. They raised two killers in a decent low crime neighborhood. I don't think that was their plan but they didn't warn us against it.

"I try not to think about it, but I wouldn't put it past them. You saw all those guns in that safe. Girl, I was terrified. My heart was racing like a horse. I didn't want my fingerprints on those things. What we did is not as worse as if the police came and found all those guns in your house and took you to jail. That's why I don't feel anything anymore. They had all that money in that safe and we have to beg our own kids for a few measly dollars for bills," Brenda stated, becoming more engulfed in her resolve.

"Don't I know, girl! We worked all our life to feed them and clothe them and keep a roof over their head and soon as they get a little money, they locking it up in a safe," Mama chimed in with her distorted logic.

"They are so ungrateful. We worked like dogs to give them a good life and look at how they treat us, girl. They probably spend more money on those fast tail girls than their own mamas," Brenda continued to speculate, make shit up, and make her self and mama believe they did the right thing. She was getting animated and really believing her hype. "They throw us a few dollars to shut us up but they aren't giving us any real money to help us. They had over $50,000 in that safe. We ain't never seen that much money in our entire lives. They probably made all that money in a day selling that shit! Shit, girl, we deserve that money for raising their ungrateful asses," Brenda concluded her rant, not knowing Khan was standing right behind her to hear that.

"Is that what you think and how you feel, Mama? Then OK!" Khan asked but it wasn't a question. He just shook his head disappointed and walked back to his room.

"Khan! I didn't mean it like that... you know I love you, right?"

CHAPTER 20

"WHAT'S UP, BABY? What are you doing?" I greeted my lady when I called to check on her.

"Nothing," Toni answered with a funky attitude.

I had no idea why she was trippin'. I brushed it off. She must have been on her period. She gets moody around that time of the month. I asked her, "What's going on tonight? Are you and the girls still going skating at World on Wheels?"

"No," Toni answered short and funky again.

My patience was starting to wear thin but I kept my composure. I took a deep breath. "So where are you going? I'm just asking so I'll know where you are and you're safe. A few fools trying to earn stripes are gunning for us right now," I said and letting her know I wasn't keeping tabs, just concerned.

She sighed like she was uninterested in what I was saying. She smacked her lips and made the beat box sound. "We going to Ultra Wave. Okay! Dang! Why you all in my business like that all of a sudden? You ain't never sweated me before. It sounds like to me that you're guilty about something."

"What?" I wasn't really asking her what the fuck she was talking about and tripping off of. I was shaken because Toni didn't even talk like that. This was not one of her episodes when she wanted Rough and Sexy Sex. I knew some shit was up. Something didn't feel right. Her next question let me know somebody was in her ear.

"What bitch were you spending our money on at Oki Dogs today, huh? And don't lie, Trav!" Toni asked me all out of character and out of pocket. Since she went there, I got into character and fed into that bullshit."

"I don't know what you're talkin' about. I wasn't with no bitch at Oki Dogs. I met Soncho up there and we had lunch. So what? I know Soncho got a big booty, but he looks nothing like a woman. I don't know who told you that."

"See? All you niggas are the same. You ain't no Mack. You're trickin', spending money on bitches at Oki Dogs. You want to know who told me that? The bitch you were trickin' on that you gave your card to with your number on it. Look, I need a man that ain't scared to tell me about some weak shit like talking to a whack bitch. I have a father, remember? And he schooled me well. If you lie about talking to a bitch, what else would you lie to me about? I don't think this is going to work out. Call me when you grow up, Trav. I need a real man." Toni hung up the phone.

Ooooh, I was pissed! I couldn't let my emotions get out of control in this situation but it was easier said than done. Toni wasn't going to be dancing at Ultra Wave tonight without me. Fuck that!

$ $ $ $

"See? What did I tell you, baby? You don't need to be with some young 19-year-old sissy that's scared to tell you he was talking to a silly bitch. All I ask of you is to just give me a chance to show you that being with me is better than that kid Trav."

Toni looked down at the card with my number on it that I gave that chick Tanya at Oki Dogs. She looked up at Pierre. "You didn't lie about it Pierre. I might consider being with you. Just give me a moment to get it together so I can come right. It wouldn't be fair to you if I came in our thang with old baggage."

"Trust me, baby. Once I pull that anaconda out, you will forget all about that little boy."

"Oh! It's like that?"

"It's definitely like that!"

"Mmm!"

$ $ $ $ $

We met up at Suge's pad. Being fly was an understatement when it pertained to my homie. He was taking it to another stratosphere. He had foreign bitches scantily dressed greeting us at the door with our favorite drinks. When I arrived, Shannon was already there. We gave each other a pound and started talking like we hadn't been feuding over the past couple of months. There was this itty-bitty gray cloud that was hovering over our friendship but it definitely wasn't going to rain on our parade. We just jumped into the current conversation and laughed at how our ages were conflicting were our grown lifestyle. Suge was just the Prom King and getting "Cutest Couple" yearbook awards a few months ago. Now he was into some other things that were fly but it wasn't any cute shit.

We all had our own cribs except for Khan, and that's only because Shannon needed him at his parents' apartment to keep an eye on his things. We had all that going on around us and we technically still had to party at the under-21 clubs. We had to laugh.

Of course, we got into good clubs ran by cats in the game 'cuz we were fly and spending money but we still liked young broads. Ultra Wave at the Veterans Auditorium was the best thing going. Ultra Wave was a cool party promotion that catered to the Westside of town. It was the opposite of what Uncle Jams Army was doing on the east side of Crenshaw. It was a party joint but they had local performers sometimes like these LA Rappers called TDF and they held these dope ass dance contests. I trip off of gangsters that try to act super hard like they're too cool to dance or don't like dancing period, and I guarantee you at least 99% of them have tried to Pop-Lock or do the

Michael Jackson at least one time in their life.

Dez rolled in shortly after me looking like a wolf that was already full but still wanted his presence to be felt near the hen house. He gave everybody a half ass handshake and hello and then just let us know what was on his mind. "What the fuck is going on out here? I come home and thought I was in the wrong spot. All I see is P-City and P-Town bullshit spray painted all over the hood bringing the property value down around here. This ain't an impoverished neighborhood, homie; they spray painting on those Jews' property. You know you can't be fucking around with those Jews' money. I know it ain't none of us spray painting. We've been past that little shit so what's going on? Are the little homies hittin' up they hood and now they're going back and forth having spray paint can and graffiti fights? This shit is making us look real raggedy. Then I asked the little homies what was up and they said we lost the war with no fight. Khan got robbed. They busted they guns at everybody. They laid a couple of us down and we haven't even fired a sling shot back at those fools. This ain't us. This ain't how we get down. This ain't Westside Gangster! Some niggas from Palms? Are you serious? What the fuck is up?" Dez looked at each of us, square in the eyes.

I stood up to answer Dez's question. "Well. First of all, Dez, it would have been nice for you to at least say hello before you started scolding us. You've been gone for a minute. We did miss your black ass but to answer your question, we had a strange little setback; we learned a lesson about greed and betrayal. And by the way, this is a cold game we chose Dez so bring a coat, muthafucka. Whew! Now. Back to my point, Dez, if we would have ended this war without letting you get a shot off we would have had to hear about this shit for the next twenty years. (mimicking Dez) *Aw fuck you muthafucka's you didn't even let me...* and all that shit so we ain't trying to hear all that. The plan I had drawn up was stolen unfortunately, but I had it memorized. We've been playing chess. Me, Soncho, and Dante got every duck lined up in a row. You know good and damn well we can't just be doing shit South Central style with that Drive-By shit in these hoods. That Westwood shit still got everybody in the city hot. You and Shannon's violent asses are the only ones that think everything is physical. We have to wait for the perfect time to get to that part of the plan, " I concluded. Now I was just as eager to get the party started as Dez, but I just didn't show it.

Dez was not trying to hear too much of what I was talking about but he also knows me and what he likes about me most is he knows there is always a method behind my madness. Even if he didn't agree with my patience, he trusted my smarts and now his only concern was his part. "So when does the damn part of the plan where it gets physical go into action?"

"Tonight!"

"A'ight."

$ $ $ $ $

We rolled up to the Veterans Auditorium in Culver City in separate cars, of course. Over half the kids there weren't driving so that made it too easy for us to take a car full of girls home after the dance and keep the one riding in the front seat overnight. I was going to have Toni in my front seat but if she trips out tonight, one of these square dancing bitches was going to get turned out real quick.

There was no need to bring our pistols to an event like Ultra Wave, plus the risk of getting caught in Culver City with them has more ramifications than actually doing a murder. We don't fuck around in Culver City. White people get pulled over by the police in Culver City so we didn't have action at nothing but breathing… if we were lucky. There were never any enemies that posed a threat at Ultra Wave Dances. Every now and then, we would see a couple of those fly niggas from Mansfield Hustlers in the house but they were always there to turn some young bitches out. If the traditional khaki-wearing Gangsters thought cats like the Mansfields and Westside dressed soft or like weirdos as they called us, they would never respect the party-crashing gangs like the KOD's Kings of Drag, the Sex Jerks, and Posers. They were definitely weirder than us. They looked more like Black Gangs from London or Great Britain or some shit. They wore their hair slicked straight back or spiked up like punkers. They wore white tee shirts and khakis tapered real narrow like cats wore in the 1960s. And they wore these English shoes up out of the United Kingdom called Creepers or Monkey Boots. They would get drunk and start fights with their rivals and crash parties. Don't take their look for weakness. A few of those weirdos were good with their boxing game, but they were not on the level of gangs like the Rolling 60's, Bloods, or Hoovers.

We weren't even on that level yet but we were right on course. All it takes is for one of their soldiers to get clipped and the party changes to a new tune. We were fighters and shooters. These guys didn't even carry knives yet so getting into a war with them was never a second thought.

We strolled in with a different swagger than the rest of the kids our age but they all knew who we were. DJ General Lee was on the turntables rocking *"You're the One for Me"* by D-Train. That shit was bumpin'. I saw the ultimate party dancer, this cutty named Kimball that belonged to this group called the Groovers in the middle of the dance floor already rocking the Party. He was sweatin' and shit but he was killing it. A little circle formed around Kimball to watch him get busy. Kimball hit a hard pause and a point and one of his dance homies in the group Todd hopped in the circle and they went into this dance called The Prep.

I've seen the dance done before but the Groovers didn't do it like everybody else. They perfected that shit. They used their hands, the lapels, and the tails on their suit jackets; they hit a shoeshine move with it and that pretty much trademarked the move as their own in my eyes.

Ultra Wave was full of girl and guy dance groups. I thought that shit was cool. There is nothing sexier to me than a woman that can get down and dance, I mean really dance and not just shaking her naked ass bumping and grinding. The Ultra Girls, the Dapper Girls, and my home girl Yaisa were a few of my favorites. Yaisa put in that work. She was another one that didn't do dance moves like everybody else. When she would hit that Guess Dance on that ass and break into her wicked cabbage patch, she would shut the whole place down. Suge liked these smooth cats called the Romeos, of course, 'cuz they were the debonair pretty boys with flair that got all the petty girls. A couple of them went to Fairfax High with us. They were known for doing this crazy move with their legs real fast called The Skate. I didn't like that dance just 'cuz I never learned how to do it. It was too much going on with that dance I couldn't understand. Jon-Jon and Malik of the Romeos had that bad boy mastered. It was wickedly great.

"Hey Trav. Hey Shannon. How are you guys doing?"

"Hey Joy! How are you?" I looked at Shannon. "You remember little Joy May Shannon? She didn't go to Saturn Elementary with us; she got to go to a good school with the uniforms and shit," I said, trying to make Shannon remember her. He didn't.

"I'm good. Are you guys staying out of trouble?" Joy asked 'cause our reputation was no mystery in this crowd.

Shannon answered truthfully. "No ma'am. We're looking for trouble. So you better get away from Trav. He has a weakness for that deep chocolate woman," Shannon said to see what reaction he would get. Joy smiled and kept it pushing. She knew what was best.

I did see this cutie pie that was worth the risk of letting Toni bust me talking to her. She had a little Janet vibe about her. She was in one of the top female dance groups, the Ultra Girls. She was a little square for my lifestyle but her tight white pants were calling me. Her coochie print in the front of those jeans was looking right. "Hey sweetheart, can I talk to you for a second?" I smiled at the little hottie. "My name is Trav. I don't know if it's your dancing, your smile, those white pants, or all three that got my attention but I know I like something about you. What's your name?

"Nickie. But everybody calls me Buttafly."

"Not Buttacup? You look so sweet and you look so edible."

"Yeah, I've been told that before." Nickie rolled her eyes. I was mad that I didn't smash on her like I normally do chicks, but I was trying not intimidate her little dancing ass. I still played the square 'cause I dug her.

"Wow! So much confidence. I like that. I like you."

"What dance group are you in?" Nickie asked me. I wanted to laugh but at the same time I felt a little left out 'cause I didn't boogie. My money, cars, and apartment didn't mean shit if I couldn't do The Guess in that crowd. So I changed the subject and pressed for the number before she asked me to dance out there. "So Buttafly, may I have your phone number so I can work on getting you to like me?"

"I really can't... right now."

"Why? Do you have a boyfriend?"

"Mmm, not yet but I'm so in love with Legend from the Soul Brothers. And there he is over there. Isn't he dreamy? Oh God! His Cutty shoulders are soooooo sexy! Sssssssss... that man! Oh that Man! Look at his dance moves... he's so smooth with his hands. His spirit is so free, Sssssssssssss whew! Go Legend! Get busy! Go Dee Daa - Love you Pa-Pa!"

I walked away from Nickie and her teen idol moment, and my homies started cracking up. I had to laugh myself. "We got to learn how to dance if we going to be coming to these kind of parties. Damn! A Gangster does not always feel welcome up in this bitch."

"Not all good girls love bad boys," Shannon expressed

"You ain't lying... but I see a few that do," Dante stated as he made a beeline toward some hoes more suitable for our lifestyle.

MCG, the house emcee, was on the microphone talking over the music and giving his sentimental shout outs while we were trying to party in that muthafucka.

"I want to give a shout out to my beautiful wife! Without her, none of these dance contests would be possible. I want to thank the Mayor of this great city for granting us the permits. Without Tom Bradley, none of this would be possible. I want to thank you for donating to the Ultra Wave Canned Good Drive because without your donation, none of this would be possible! I want to give a shout out to Martin Luther King 'cuz without his dream, I would have never met my beautiful wife, and without my beautiful wife..."

"We know nigga, life would be impossible! Now turn on the music back on..." Soncho yelled and caused a roar of laughter from our little section, but MCG continued with his testimony.

The night was mad young. It wasn't even ten o'clock yet. We never get to parties that early but we had been cooped up ever since the P-Town attacks so it was time we came out and let things breathe.

As the night moved on, my Westside Crew enjoyed the evening talking to the ladies and checking out the good stage shows that was worth watching to us. Some dance groups performed. I'm not sure if it was a dance contest and we really didn't pay attention to the details; it was just part of the scene to us. Those dance groups were very similar to gang culture without the extreme violence. They banged the names of their dance crews all night. A lot of them didn't like each other and exchanged mad stares. They battled each other to see who was the best. They took each other's boyfriends and girlfriends. If the group lost badly, it showed weakness. You didn't want to be seen leaving with a dancer that came in last place.

Shannon and Dante were chilling against the wall with grins on their face as they watched the girl groups battle each other to this song by Lisa Lisa & Cult Jam. I think it was called "Don't Stop!"

We weren't sure, but that was our favorite part of the record. General Lee would cut that part of the record back and forth on the turntables and the girls would break loose on that song. Shannon was the worst dancer in our crew only 'cuz we wanted to boogie so badly. When he did the basic two-step or slow danced or The Freak when it was hot, he was good. When he tried to do the Guess, and the Prep and Cha-Cha, or anything in open space, he had problems adjusting.

This older dude we knew named Chris approached them, shook their hands and spoke. "Hey! What's up Shannon? ...Dez....Suge, the young playa...Khan...Dante.... Soncho! You looking good. You finally lost that baby fat and looking grown. You look good, boy!" The thing that tripped us out about some of the older cats that had money from illegal activity was we never knew how they got it.

Dope is all over the country right now. That is what I'm labeled as and will probably be forever remembered as a dope dealer, even though I have my hands in other ventures. The OGs from our hood have no labels. I couldn't say that was a good thing 'cause it's not like it helps them stay low key. They catch cases and go to jail like everybody else so somebody knows what they're doing but we just never did.

Chris was with this white boy that looked like he was hardened by the game or had his hand in it. His name was Brandon. He lived in Bel Air. He dressed liked a surfer white boy but his clothes were new and pressed. Most surfers have the fashionably wrinkled or fresh out of the dryer look. He wore jewelry instead of puka shells, too. He had on a very nice watch that you wouldn't see on the average white dude.

"What are you high rollin' players doing in here with all these little kids? Y'all gonna fuck around and catch a case messing with these young broads, but shit, I'm about to fuck around and catch one. These little freaks are fine as hell!" Chris said as he looked around rubbing his chest with the back of his right hand. He always talked with one foot in front of the other.

"What the hell you talking about? None of us are over 19 and Khan is still in high school. What the hell are YOU doing in here? You coming to check on your kids?" Dez clowned Chris for fucking with us. Dez liked Chris but never respected his hustle 'cause he never shared knowledge about the game with us coming up.

"Aww, cut that out. You know I ain't that old to be having kids in this muthafucka but I'm going to fuck around and make some kids tonight up in here. Damn! You dudes are still in your teens and rolling around in Corvettes and shit? When I was 19, I had a Brown Celica that leaked oil. You little dudes be out here doing your thing, huh?"

"We do a little something-something, but not like you. You been having money for years," Shannon stated.

"And what brings you here looking like the two muthafuckas from Miami Vice, making people think the police is up in here," Soncho roasted Chris, who dressed in some loose pants, with no socks and Le Glove Slip On Shoes, and a colored tank top underneath a light pink blazer, while he subliminally put the White Boy on the spot to see what he was about.

Brandon looked at Chris' outfit and said, "Mmm. See, I told you this would happen if you wore that Miami Vice get-up in public, dude! Totally not cool!"

Chris grinned. "Good one, Baby Fat, but we are up here checking out the space in the different rooms. Brandon is helping put on this fundraiser for his father's non-profit organization."

"Ahh, y'all are making that *Save the Whales* money, huh? I heard that's almost better than Church money." Dez just threw that out there to see if they were legit or if they would bite. They half assed laughed it off and started looking around the venue.

"This is the biggest room here. Those other two were smaller than this. What do you think, Brandon?" Chris asked, totally ignoring Dez's question.

"It's bigger. This will work fine. It will definitely hold the amount of people we will be inviting." Brandon seemed satisfied with what he came to see.

"Excuse me, Brandon, but is your last name Beaton?" Dante asked. Suge raised his antennas when he heard the name.

"Yeah. How did you know? Have we met before? You kinda look familiar."

"We hung out a few times and played when we were little. I used to come to those campaign dinners at your house with my mom," Dante tried to make Brandon remember.

"Oh yeah. I kind of remember. That was a long time ago," Brandon stated as he tried to go down memory lane but it was vague. Brandon had seen more Black People than we had Whites as kids. Interacting with white folks when we were young was like an event. We discussed what the experience was like with family and friends. Older family members would kind of piss us off because they always thought we were doing something special because white folks accepted us. Shannon was the first one in our crew hanging with white boys that introduced us to cocaine and the pill game. They are not to blame for us being in the game but they aren't the perfect angels society portrays them to be. And it's true they are not human. Whitey is something else.

"Small world. Hey Brandon, since you guys are familiar with each other you might want to reconnect and reminisce about old times and discover that you may still have common interest today," Chris winked at Brandon along with a nod. Then he continued and flipped the conversation toward us. "But hey. What's going on in the neighborhood? The streets said some new crew has been punking y'all all over the city? And that ain't me talking. That's the streets."

"You at the Dead End with that one, Player. I haven't heard no shit like that. You see us here right? You can answer that question for yourself," Dez stated agitated. He didn't like our name being tainted in the streets like that. It was bad for business.

"Well, it ain't my business, but somebody needs to handle that. The neighborhood is looking raggedy with gang writing on the walls. My mother lives over there. What the hell is P-City? Playboy Gangster Crips?"

"No, homie, this new Hustler Crew over in the Palms district kicking up a little dust; that's all."

"Palms? Are they white boys?"

"No, they're Black. A lot Mixed Breed, light-skinned Niggas and a few... I don't know what the fuck they are, Egyptian or Armenian but they ain't Black."

"You gangsters raised in good homes is some dangerous shit. I understand though. Our parents raised us in good surroundings but didn't teach us what it took to maintain the lifestyle they made for us. Our parents didn't come up taking the College route. They had to be clever and jump on opportunities when they presented themselves. But hey, I'm not here for a sermon. We just came to check the joint out. We have another soiree we have to attend later on tonight. Make sure you exchange numbers with Brandon and get with us once that street shit y'all into is over. Hey, give your boy Trav some dap for me, and we'll see you players soon."

"What people do for Money!" What people do for moneeeyyyyy...?"

$ $ $ $ $

"I can't believe every hotel in LA is sold out. This is crazy."

"I know and this is taking up all of our quality time looking for a room, Pierre. You know I have to be back at the dance before it's over," Toni stated after she gave in to Pierre's advances.

"I know baby, but you said you won't go to a motel. C'mon Toni, I mean if we just fly down Venice and hit the Seaway Mo-Mo, do our thing, and we will be back in no time," Pierre begged Toni to go beneath her standards.

Toni looked at Pierre out of the side of her neck like he was crazy. She rolled her eyes and said, "I do not go to hood rat heaven. You have to come better than that if you want some of this good loving," Toni stated as her pager went off. It was me calling her, 911-911. She sighed with her mouth open and rolled her eyes to the top of her head. She mumbled, *"This nigga is getting on my nerves. I wish his lying ass would stop calling me."*

"Is that the Buster again? What that fool want now? I heard you tell him to kick rocks. He don't want to let you go. I don't blame him but he's playing himself. You want me to call him back for you and tell him you're with me now. You know he don't want no more problems with P-Town," Pierre suggested to keep the ball rolling.

"Nah, it's cool. He'll go away eventually." Toni said ready to change the subject.

"Okay cool. I think that would be best for him. Well, it's a cool inn a few miles from Beverly Hills. Are you all right with that?" Pierre tried to put on his nice voice so he wouldn't blow his opportunity to fuck my woman.

"I have to see it first but I guess that's cool only 'cuz I really want you to hit this. My Panties are already wet." Toni reached down real sexy and put her hand in her panties. She moaned and moved two fingers in a circular motion across her clit and it made a squishing sound as her wetness soaked against the front of her sexy panties. She said, "Can you hear that? My pussy wants you."

Pierre stepped on the gas a little harder and put some speed to his ride. They arrived at the Dunes Inn on Wilshire in record time. It was closer to Crenshaw than Beverly Hills but since it was on Wilshire and it looked clean Toni was cool with it. Pierre hopped out of the car praying there was a vacancy. It sells out on the weekends a lot. They had one room left.

But that was a good and bad thing. Good it was a vacancy; bad 'cause it was going to be costly. The last room on a weekend when they know sex is on the line costs double and that's the minimum. Pierre had to dish out $200 plus the tax for a quickie and he did not like that. It was his burning desire to fuck my woman better than me then cum in her mouth or on her face to degrade and disrespect my name in the streets. He truly did like Toni, any man would, but his clouded vision caused him to forget that. He initially wanted Toni to be with him but the pressure of his homeboys along with satisfying *their* egos had him thinking sick with his dick.

Pierre didn't even come all the way back to the car. He came far enough for Toni to see him flagging her to come on with a half grin-half pissed smirk on his face. "C'mon baby! C'mon!" Pierre held up the room key and jiggled it. Toni was taking her time getting out of the car.

"Hold on! I have to fix myself. You got me a little messy," Toni stated real sexy and blew Pierre's ego through the roof.

They were in room 206. They took the stairs up one flight. "We barely got this room baby. The old Jew at the desk said some poor sucker rented it and their date didn't show up. It sure sucks to be him, right? Kind of like how your boy Trav is going to feel once…" Pierre got ahead of himself and broke off his sentence hoping Toni didn't hear that last part. Toni heard him but she let it slide.

Pierre opened the room door and hurried in. He took a quick peek and checked the bathroom and the closet out of habit. Pierre sat his gun on the nightstand. The room smelled a little stale. It had a couple of black spots on the carpet but overall it was cool for the occasion. Pierre turned the lights off but Toni turned the desk lamp back on. She said, "I want to see that Big Dick you have been bragging about on the phone so much. I want to see it and hold it, feel it in my mouth and then fill my pussy up with all of it."

"Oh, you're a freak. I like that shit!" Chris said excited and began to undress fast. Toni stared undressing slowly. He stopped at his pants and tried to take Toni's bra off. He was dying to see those perfect breasts that looked so good under her shirts. Toni pushed him back off of her and grabbed his belt buckle and loosened it.

Pierre's manhood hadn't started rising yet. He felt uncomfortable because Toni was still in charge and in control. She unhooked his pants and let them drop to the floor. She got down on her knees and placed her fingertips on the elastic waistband of his boxers. She started pulling them down slowly. As his manhood slowly started becoming exposed, Toni gasped like it was the most beautiful thing in this world, just like that *and it gets in ya*. She screamed, "Oh my God! Oh shit! Look at the big ass dick. Oh fuck… There's more? Damn!" She said as she stayed on her knees wide-eyed.

Pierre was asshole naked, and Toni was still in her pants and bra. She opened her mouth for Pierre to put his dick in it. He lifted it up and put it near her lips, and Toni stood up. Pierre tried to put his hand around her head and pull her back down but she pushed him back hard again. Toni kept pushing him until he fell back on the bed. He hurt his tailbone a little when he fell back on the thin mattress but he didn't show it.

"You know what turns me on the most? I like to play with my pussy while a man jack his big dick off until it gets so hard I want it in my mouth. Then I want him to put it in me so I can ride it until you make me cum all over it," Toni explained as she popped open the button on her pants and took them down slowly over her curvaceous hips. That sweet gap between Toni's thighs started making Pierre's blood pressure rise. He laid all the way back on the bed and started stroking his shaft. Toni stood at the foot of the bed. She moved her panties to the side and started rubbing her clit and eased her middle finger in the hole. She moaned.

Pierre started jacking his dick faster and harder. It began to grow into a full-blown erection and he asked, "Is my dick bigger than Trav?"

"Ten times bigger. I don't even know how I'm going to take a pounding from that entire dick. It looks big like a mammer. Damn

Pierre! You are all man, baby. I'm about to ride that big monster like a Roller Coaster. Keeping stroking it baby, ooh its almost there where I want it. I'm going crazy! Keep stroking that dick baby just like that. Ahhhh! Yes, keep stroking it!"

"Is that how you like me to do it?"

"Oh YES! YES! Jack it hard -just like that!

"Yeah?"

"YES, BABY! I want to ride it!"

"Yeah?"

"YEAH NIGGA!"

BOOP!

BOOP!

BOOP!

BOOP!

I pressed that Smith and Wesson .500 Magnum and blew four manholes through that nigga's back and out his chest through that old thin mattress. All the air left his body and his bowels moved. The motel room immediately started smelling like shit. He was stinking up the whole room. I was underneath his dead ass and only a thin mattress stood between us. I rolled out from underneath the bed. Toni had her cute little .25 that packed a lot of power in her hand standing over me. She raised her hand and then popped two in Pierre's head for insurance.

"Even with that hand cannon you got, I just don't trust body shots, baby. My daddy taught me that when I was a little girl. But damn, that gat is huge, baby! What that hell is that?"

"That's a Magnum .500, I like this muthafucka. When I pull this bad boy out, fools is going to know I came to do damage."

"Shit, more than that!" Toni grinned.

The thought hit me hard. *Pierre wanted to fuck my woman! Ain't that a bitch!* I raised my Magnum to blow his face off and Toni raised her hand and froze my next shot. She shook her head to let me know it wasn't necessary.

While Toni was getting herself situated, there was a light knock on the door. Two double taps, "Tap-tap… tap-tap!" Toni's eyes got big as hell. She froze and stood still. I whispered through the door, "Amigo?"

"Si."

I opened the door and two border brothers came in with their tools ready to work. My homie Amigo did disposal work and magic 'cause he was known to make shit disappear forever. He had a name but we just called each other Amigo.

"How much to make all this go away, Amigo?" I asked 'cause the price is always different but it's always low.

"$250," he answered.

$250? Damn Amigo, y'all really do work below minimum wage. Do you have familia?"

"Ahh si, mucho grande!"

"Take these pesos, Amigo, and split that shit up," I hit them off with like $1,500. Amigo's little Mexican partner that I didn't know started crying. I ain't never seen a muthafucka get that happy over that amount of money. They kept hugging me and calling me Santo Martin.

Now I ain't on no homo stuff and I know it was some punk ass shit, but that male ego is a muthafucka sometimes and it got the best of me. As we were walking out of the room I had to look back to see what Pierre was packin'. Toni was sounding a little too believable when I was hiding under the bed. I almost bite a hole through my lip when she was talking like that and it was *My Plan*! I just kind of positioned my body in a way so it would look like I was checking on Amigo one last time but I shot a quick glance at the shaft, still in hand.

I smiled. Pierre wasn't working with nothing. My baby was just playing the part and feeding his ego. I still slipped and showed my adolescence and blurted, "His dick is not bigger than mine!"

Toni shook her head like she was embarrassed to be next to me at that moment because of my silly statement. "Men! You guys think of the craziest shit at the most inopportune times. Men and your fucking egos, my gosh!" Toni exclaimed as she walked ahead of me not believing she just heard that after we just put Pierre in a deep sleep and set his soul free.

"'Hey, I'm 19 and that shit still means something. I needed to know!" I stated and we stared laughing.

Toni kept it real though. "Trust me if his dick was all that he wouldn't have died with it in *his* hand! You can believe that."

$ $ $ $ $

Toni and I showed up back to Ultra Wave Together. I missed the Dance Contest. The Groovers won the Big Trophy. Shannon said they were on stage rippin' that bad boy up! Shit, that was the same thing Amigo and his compadre was doing to Pierre with Slick Moves but they were far less exciting than doing The Prep.

Shannon was ready to walk out of the door when he saw Toni and I walking in. We still had some time before the party ended so Toni and I got our groove on. My crew saw that look in my eye and was ready to execute the rest of the plan. Toni and I didn't say a word. They could just feel that hot energy and adrenaline rush we brought back, but we were just as cool and calm to anybody else that saw us.

I won't lie. I was ready to see what my Magnum .500 could really do. Now I just don't want to shoot a villain just because I had a new toy that was so fuckin' awesome—that's how dope the gun was, it changed my speech pattern—but I really just wanted to see the look on a fool's face when I pulled that big bad boy out in a gun fight. I know fa-sho that half my battle, if not all of it, will be won without letting off one shot. We were all eager to get the real party started, but we still had a little time to *kill* before it became a literal thang.

CHAPTER 21

"WHAT TIME IS IT? This fuckin' white boy got me waiting out here in Pan Pacific Park at midnight for his stringy haired ass. I told him I didn't like waiting… especially with fucking a half a bird in the open. This ain't good business, White Boy! He's starting to do that nigga shit! Damn, It's dark as fuck out here tonight!" Reggie Duero from the Palm City Hustlers complained as he waited for his *rich white boy*, the name he always called Joey in front of everybody to impress them he was getting white money.

But the last time we all checked, money was green. His type of Uncle Tom thinking was a justifiable reason to remove him from Earth, plus he was a buster.

Reginald Duero was a black dude that grew up in Pacific Palisades. I don't even have to describe him. His name and area lets you know he's a high yellow nigga with sandy brown hair that's curly and course. He was a spoiled cocky son of a bitch that shouldn't even be in the game, but his style of living took currency. His family was comfortable but they didn't have liquid cash to splurge. They would buy him a Porsche but he had to maintain its upkeep as well as those expensive white chicks that liked only cocaine that he fucked with.

Joey's BMW pulled up in the dark parking lot with the bright lights on. It was parked fifteen yards directly behind Reginald's Porsche. Reginald and Joey always did Trunk-to-Trunk exchanges with the coke and the money when it was a Hit & Split transaction like tonight. They trusted each other and the goods were always right. Reginald got out of car bitching because Joey was late and covered his eyes with the side of his forearm.

"This is a Porsche, my friend. The Trunk is in the front of the car Mr. BMW Man. You should have pulled in and parked sideways if you are trying to help provide some light," Reginald babbled as he walked to the front of his car and popped the trunk. Reginald peeped to the side and saw Joey and two other white dudes he'd seen before walking towards him with a knapsack being held by the drawstrings.

Reginald let his guard all the way down. He had his little .25 in the stash box but it was nowhere near him. Reginald didn't need that firearm. These weren't niggas from the hood that did *that Nigga Shit*, that phrase he used on a consistent basis. These were just a couple of skinny rich white dudes in cargo shorts that couldn't possibly be a threat. They didn't want any problems. That's how Reginald always thought until Joey's skinny friend threw that sack over his head and wrapped that drawstring around his neck.

They bopped him over the head with a club and he dropped to the concrete. They cuffed his hands behind his back and tied his feet together. They lifted his body and stuffed his ass in the trunk with the spare tire still in. That was most uncomfortable.

Joey was white but he also sold dope and hung out with other beach boys that weren't into surfing. Joey was the one that exposed us to the power of the coca plant. We had been playing this Reginald character for a minute now. We had him thinking he stole Shannon's best customer. Joey spent a little throw money and some bad counterfeits mixed in as a way to bait that fool.

We crept out from behind the trees in the park like spooks in the night. We shook hands with Joey and his crew and told them we would settle business later. They knew we were good for it.

They hopped back in Joey's BMW and drove away. Dante got behind the wheel of Reginald's Porsche. Dez hopped in the passenger seat. They took Reginald Duero for a long uncomfortable drive with a spare tire and jack pressed hard up against his back. They returned within the hour but Reginald Duero was never seen on Earth again.

$ $ $ $

Shannon waited patiently in the bushes in front of the apartment building of the Palm boy that shot at his brother Khan for over four hours. I always commended Shannon for his discipline in situations where he had to stay low key in the cut.

I remember when he got caught in a situation a while back. I can't remember if it was a drug sweep or if they were looking for a fugitive or for his crazy ass, but the entire neighborhood was blocked off. Helicopters were flying overhead. The *"somebody is going to jail today"* Police were out deep. You know the ones that come in jeans, tight tee shirts, and bulletproof vests, and the other half are wearing windbreakers on top of the same ensemble.

That day, Shannon crept through a vent under Mr. Jones' house and stayed there for at least eight hours. Shannon said he would have stayed there for two days if he had to. He said he had some weed in his pocket so he was cool. That was also Shannon's M.O. when he hits a fool solo. He likes to come out of a dark hiding spot and lick off that kill shot. *Boom*! They never see it coming. Like now.

That Palm Boy that shot at Khan rolled up to his apartment around 3:30 in the morning like any other weekend. There is no need to say his name because he's not even going to make it out of this paragraph. Palm Boy had his McDonalds bag and his keys in one hand and his 9mm in the other. He looked up and down the street as he traveled up his walkway to enter the building. Palm Boy had nothing on his mind but sinking his teeth into that Filet O Fish sandwich.

That's a weak-ass way to spend your last moments on Earth: thinking about sinking your teeth into a Filet O Fish Sandwich. Shannon snatched that kid's life away and he never saw it coming. The McDonalds bag dropped to the concrete and Shannon looked at it as he drug the dead body into the bushes. He said, "Better me than that shit you were about to eat. That McDonalds would have killed you eventually—slow and painfully. I did you a favor." Swine-eating Shannon had the nerve to say that to the corpse before he buried it in the hole we made a week before. No, we didn't have a shovel to dig a big ass hole like you see Mafia cats do in the movies. We didn't have time for all that shit. We made it big enough to drop him and cover him with dirt and lime to kill the smell for a couple of days.

These first three hits we put down were on the Palm Boys that would be a threat later on down the line. These weren't the disrespectful, loud Palm Tree Busters that had been kicking up all that dust. They needed to be dealt with in a different way all together. We had something special in store for those bitch ass niggas. These other chumps were a decent second string that could play with the starters in this game. What we couldn't do is alert the starting five that three of their soldiers were eliminated. They would go into hiding and we would miss our opportunity.

Everything was calculated. I had started planning all these tactics weeks before we left for New York. I knew where they lived, where their girlfriends lived, their mamas and where they worked. I even saw that fool Pierre watching me talk to his broad in front of Oki Dogs. Her friends kept looking up the street like a boyfriend was about to bust them for talking to another man. I didn't even have to turn around and look. Their body language and facial expressions told me everything I needed to know. I knew what type of dude Pierre was so it was the perfect opportunity for Toni and I to bond on a different level. Toni's father must gave her mad game coming up or it was just in her naturally because when I approached her with the plan she offered suggestions and came up with the idea of making sure it was only one motel room available in LA. That was some slick shit. It cost us a little money but it worked to a tee.

Toni handled business unbelievably well. I could tell that wasn't the first time she'd been in a situation that involved firearms and a soul being released. It made me wonder what her and Pops were really in to coming up.

$ $ $ $ $

With the ones that would have been next in line eliminated, it was time to chop the head off those snakes that had been slithering through our hood. This shit was business and personal. They wanted a rep by so-called terrorizing the hood they didn't own. We wanted something they had from day one and we were about to obtain it and gain full ownership. It was time for the Young Locs on the Westside to grow up and put in that Big Man's work. Tool up! Let's get 'em!

Those disrespectful five from Palm City met up at Kenyan's house on the 2600 block of Carmona right there off of Adams. It was a real small two-bedroom house that his parents rented out to him when they moved to a bigger home in Hesperia. New affordable homes sent a lot of middle class couples looking for a quiet area to live in packing out of the old neighborhoods. His parents did well for themselves but as they were getting closer to retirement, they could get more bang for their buck and have a better chance to live happily ever after moving to the High Desert. Kenyan's parents knew he was too young to turn the deed to the house over to him at this time but his father did leave the Billiards Bar in Santa Monica in his goofy ass son's name. It didn't lose money but it didn't make much either.

His pops was not a street dude so he didn't see the value in it and only had it because he bought it at a good price a long time back. However, I saw a gold mine and I wanted it. Kenyan was too stupid to have ownership of something that required a brain to operate. It was in a prime location, too. Kenyan used it as a hangout spot and only had one person working the bar on the payroll. The Asian Pool Sharks and gamblers had money to burn. Kenyan's dumb ass didn't even see it. I also had a gut feeling Kenyan left his treasures hiding there. Money, drugs, guns, or something of value was stashed there. I just felt it. He just seems like he's that type.

It was around 11:30am. Those Palm Tree bitches just left The Pancake House in Westchester off of Manchester and showed up at Kenyan's for a meet. Kenyan lived in Marvin Gangster Crip hood but his pops kept him away from the local thugs. He sent him to a good, culturally balanced school where he learned to be more devious and scandalous than if he were crippin' in his own hood. The P-City Boys were lounging around smoking weed and feeling full from eating all those pancakes and eggs. They had just woke up two hours before and were already ready for a nap after that. Too many pancakes and some cheap weed is the blueprint for a lazy day. They were sitting around the house feeling too relaxed. The *Itis* had already kicked in. A couple of them were sitting in front of the TV playing video games, one was on the phone, another one was half dozing off, but in the midst of all that going on all of them were talking shit about us, even the one half asleep. He was talking shit with his eyes closed cuddled up in the corner of the couch.

"We gonna bring it to these Westside niggas. I'm gonna Hand Clap that punk Shannon myself. I'm gonna bring it to that fool crazy!"

"You heard from Pierre? Stephan asked as he took a long drag from the cigarette he just lit after hitting the joint that was in rotation. He believed the cigarette boosted his high. It did give him a little head rush.

"Pierre is somewhere fucking Trav' broad right now, swell," Kenyan blurted and caused everybody to laugh.

"Damn, he peeled that quick. I want that Sweet fags broad. What's his name? *Sugars*? That sounds like he's a bitch!" Bullet sarcastically mimicked Suge's name and caused another hefty size laugh from all the Palm Boys in the room. Oh, they were getting a kick out of dissing us. It was feeling better than sex.

Kenyan said, "Call that fool Duero and see where he is with that money. What time is it? Anybody got a watch?

"I got this nice one on this buster from…? Wait. What was the name of that faggot gang again? Westside Gay Blades? Well that buster's watch says 11:43," Bullet Ze' bragged and kept them laughing. His was cracking ribs with all his jokes.

"Hit that fool Reggie up right now. He's slowing me up. I got shit to do!" Kenyan stated like he was agitated.

"Shit, all those Pancakes you had ain't letting you do a damn thing no time soon. That button around your waist is screaming right now. Your pants are getting tighter as I'm speaking."

"You ain't bullshittin', Bullet." Kenyan unloosened that top button on his flooding 501 Jeans and blew air out of his mouth soon as he felt that relief. He flopped on the couch with that happy/sleepy look on his face. Kenyan wanted to be the leader so bad and saw himself as that, but LA hustler gangs didn't get down like that. We were all independent contractors that ran together in crews that usually turned into gangs eventually from an unwanted circumstance. Kenyan was talking but nobody was moving. "Y'all just be leaving weed all out in the open. Clean that shit up before you get all of us pinched."

Everybody in the room stopped what they were doing and looked at Kenyan like he was crazy. Homie with his eyes closed even raised his head up for a second. Those fools had enough cash, drugs, and hot guns with bodies on them stashed in that house to build an effective case against them that would stick for sure. The police wouldn't even mention the weed in their report. It would be inadmissible. They just waved off his crazy talk. They all turned back around slow and went back to what they were doing.

Kenyan wasn't giving up his leadership position that easy. He got back to business. "It's going down tonight! Soon as Pierre finish fucking the shit out of Trav' broad, she's going to give up the address to his pad. We gonna ice that bitch Toni, too. I don't like bitches like that. She gave that nigga Trav up for getting a phone number from a silly bitch. He didn't even get the draws. Now she don't care if he gets murdered and she justified it by saying *well he shouldn't have been plotting to cheat on me,* and calling it karma. That ain't karma— that's premeditated revenge, bitch. What happened to breaking up and telling a muthafucka *I don't want to go with you anymore.* Remember that shit in school? Those words hurt like hell when you heard them. But yeah man, I can't have no broads like that around me. I hope Pierre enjoyed it. That's a one hit 'em and quit 'em for real. Now that nigga Shannon, I'm killing him slow. That's personal."

"I want all those busters but those ain't the ones we need to worry about. What we gonna do about that fool Dez? He's the killer." Bullet was concerned.

Kenyan answered, "Oh, we're killing him first. He's the most dangerous. Any opportunity we have to catch him slippin', he got to go. I don't fuckin' care if it's broad daylight in church. We hit Dez and leave him laid out in the street and those other fags will…"

POP!

Dez shot the nigga that was sleeping on the couch and finished Kenyan's sentence for him, "Will what? Run up in your crib and catch you slippin' like a muthafucka?"

We all stood in Kenyan's crib, relaxed with our guns by our sides. The unexpected gunshot spooked those other fools and had them out of character. They were scared now—not like punks, they had been in shootouts and killed before—but they had never been in this type of situation, a no-winner. They had guns in the house within their reach that they couldn't grab. It was a terrible situation for them to be in. Khan and Soncho confiscated the weapons that were out in the open and checked their persons as well.

I don't know what triggered the beast in Khan but none of us saw what was coming next. This nigga pulled out a Machete from the small of his back, raised it high and came down hard across Bullet's forearm and he chopped that muthafucka clean off.

"That's my watch. I want it back," Khan stated. Bullet lost his wrist so fast he didn't even feel it until he saw it roll on the floor in front of him and all his homeboys gasped. Bullet went into shock after seeing that. Bullet had nothing else to lose. He wasn't about to faint at the sight of his own blood and hand on the floor; he was about to go berserk and lose it. Shannon had to kill him because he was about to become a danger to us all.

Shannon looked at his brother. He was pleased in a sense that the wolf came out of his brother, but at the same time he still had to school him. "What the fuck is you doing Khan? You can't be just *removing* limbs. We ain't in El Salvador. That's mayhem. That carries life in Prison. That watch wasn't that nice."

"Principles," Khan said and stared at homeboy who had been playing video games with his nostrils flaring up and out from his hard breathing. Homeboy sat his joystick down and remained still. Damn. Khan stole the thunder from my Magnum surprise. The shocked look he put on their faces was what I was trying to achieve.

I walked over to Kenyan. He was the main one trying to take us out and now we were in his house with Dez's gun in his mouth. I gave Dez the nod and he removed the barrel from his tonsils. I wanted to have a nice conversation with that guy. He was real rude that last time we talked in the Roscoe's parking lot. I have an excellent memory bank. Kenyan still tried to control what was going to happen. Dez should have left his gun in his mouth 'cuz he wasn't talking about nothing.

"OK. You caught us slippin', y'all got that. Give yourselves a hand. Now commit your little robbery or whatever the fuck you came to do and get on. Enjoy this money while you can 'cause you won't have it long."

I frowned my face up to let him know it wasn't that simple. "We didn't come for that Kenyan. We're leaving that *on the table*." I knew he didn't know what that term meant but he would be educated on it soon enough.

"Well, what the fuck do you want then?" Kenyan asked with a funky attitude.

Suge handed me a dark green file folder with a string fastener. I unwound the string from around the circular disc. I pulled out the deed to his billiards joint and necessary paperwork for Kenyan to transfer ownership over to me. He was confused. Kenyan wasn't prepared for this level of the game. He thought being a gangster was all about spray-painting walls, doing drive-bys, and selling dope.

Kenyan knew there was only one place we could have gotten that deed. He saw his father's signature on it that was backdated properly to clear us of any foul play. He didn't want to believe that his silly behavior sent Suge, Soncho, and myself to his parents' nice new home way out in Hesperia. There was no way we had the discipline and determination to drive that far. We must have connections downtown or something.

"What is this?" Kenyan asked not sure what was really happening. His father gave him the property, but he was too young and unorganized to keep the paperwork. His father still handled all that and didn't bother teaching him.

"I need your signature right there on that line, and I need you to sign and initial these papers here so I can get that pool hall up out of you. I heard you were having trouble with paying the property tax on it." I lied about the taxes but he didn't know.

"So let me get this right. All you want is that funky pool hall but none of this money in here?" Kenyan asked again eager like he wanted to make that deal but it was a silly con. "Fuck you. I ain't giving you shit! You got to take anything you want from me. You better take that little cash over there and use that money to move out of your mama's house before you lose another bitch behind it, little boy... How's Toni doing?"

"What you say, nigga?"

"Oh. You didn't know my homie Pierre has been fucking your

woman good, long dick style all night long… fucking her all in the ass, nuttin' in her mouth so unless you want him to ship that bitch back to you not looking like her normal self, I think its best for you to be leaving now. You are done here. Thought you were doing something real gangster, didn't you? Sneaking in here, shootin' a sleeping man, and cutting off fingers like the Mafia. Man, get the fuck out of my house before I make the call to Pierre and tell him to make it so Toni won't like it as much."

"Call him," I said with an even and low voice.

Kenyan didn't know how to take that statement. I realized then he had real trouble with denial.

"Call him… I doubt if he answers though…" I paused for a moment and then continued. "The coldest part about that whole ordeal was Pierre never got a chance to get that nut off. If it wasn't my woman, I would have felt a little bad for him. Damn! Look at your face. All your leverage is gone. Now, like I was saying, I need your signature here and here, and your initials right here." This time I pointed to the blank lines on the paper with my Magnum. .500. I still didn't get the effect I was hoping for. My own homies were in awe of it more than the Palm Trees feared getting cut down by it.

"I told you I wasn't signing shit. You think killing Pierre is supposed to make me change my mind. That was my homie and I'll miss him, but fuck you and that signature. Go sit down somewhere, little boy, and let me talk to Dez."

"You are one disrespectful little bastard, ain't you? Caroline said you'd always been hardheaded. Oh, you didn't know? I finally moved out of my mama's house and I moved in with your mama… way out in Hesperia. Let me ask you something, Kenyan. Have you ever seen your mama naked since you've been grown?" I asked as I dropped a Polaroid picture on his lap of his naked mama's 55 year-old body.

"Look at your mama's titties touching her waistline with that loose belly fat in the way." I walked over to the other Palm Boy Stephan and dropped a picture of Kenyan's naked mama in front of him, too, and said, "You ever wonder what Kenyan's mama look like with her clothes off? Here she is, asshole naked... look at that, would you hit that? Look at that figure. That shit don't make no sense."

"Aww, c'mon man! That looks terrible! Get that out..." Stephan cut off his sentence when he realized it was his homie's mama he was talking about. He didn't even mean for it to come out like that. I gave a picture to each one in the room. They all turned their nose up and twisted their face when they saw her naked.

"I can't believe your daddy got to come and hit that every night after working hard all day. Now I see why your daddy is on the bottle so hard. That's the kind of body that makes married men solicit prostitutes. That's a damn shame... Oh, now you don't want to see this picture, you ain't going to like this one bit. I got my dick out. Now wait—let's get something straight. Don't get all shook up thinking I raped that bitch so get that shit out your mind. That's your father's pussy and I do not want that... but she did though. You wanna see the way she is looking at the head in this picture? I've never met a woman in my life that was offended that we weren't there to rape her." I paused and looked each of him in the eyes. "Did you know you mama is an old freak? Now listen. We got the homie out in Hesperia right now waiting for our call. Don't do your mama like that. She don't deserve no harm coming to her because of her silly ass son. Do the right thing." I had lied about the picture with his mom and me to make him sweat a little bit more. I'm glad he didn't call my bluff.

Kenyan signed the paperwork. Dez tied his hands behind his back. Shannon took Khan's knife and slid it real slow across his throat. His neck split open so wide his big head dropped backwards and it was hanging on by the skin. Dez lifted it by the hair and put one shot in the back of his head. Dez was superstitious like Toni. He had to know for sure. We picked off the remaining Palm tree punks and tied them up. We looked around at the carnage and our plan was perfectly executed.

The statement we sought to make got no better than this. Shannon even turned the fish tank over on the floor. We didn't leave anything breathing.

When the streets hear about this hit, they are going to know we are not to be played with. By leaving all the money, drugs and guns the Palm Tree Boys had at the house *On the Table,* our message is going to read loud and clear. That's how all the old mobs and big time gangsters did it when a rival gang was out of pocket. Kill all them muthafuckas and leave everything on the table. Even when the police see it they are going to automatically chalk it up as a personal gang retaliation hit, make themselves look good on the news with the drug and guns, and walk away with the money they failed to report. It was an unwritten gangster code that's been in play for years. We want to play with the big boys. It was our time. *Westside Gangster Mack! Fool!* We threw our set up and then shook the spot the same way we snuck in.

$ $ $ $ $

LATER THAT NIGHT...

Around midnight I put on some dark clothes and hopped in my car. Leaving all that money on the table to make a statement had been bothering me ever since we left it. It sounded real gangster when we strategized the plan and I know in my heart it was the right thing to do but in my soul, the Fatback Band was playing *"Money... got to get my hands on some."* That's Italian mob shit. I'm not there yet. We are Young Locs on the Westside trying to come up around this muthafucka and niggas can't be leaving no free money on the table. I was going to divide it with my homies without question but I was also going to suggest we invest in something legal or illegal until we flip it, and then look into business ventures. I had to get that bread or

I would never be able to sleep.

I crept slowly through the back window. The entire house was dark except for a thin streak of moonlight that eased through the slight crack in the drapes. I didn't need light. That money was calling me. The mental picture I took of the room that kept showing itself in my head since we left the money behind helped a little, too. I felt around the table where one of the duffle bags was located and it wasn't there.

I got nervous. I pulled my Big Bad Boy out and dropped to the floor. I figured that if anybody were going to shoot in the dark, the first shot wouldn't be aimed at the floor. I crawled on my belly to the area where the other bag was located near the couch. It was there. Now I was confused. This shit was fucking with my mind. I crawled on my belly to the other side of the couch where the last money bag was located and it was there, but next to it was the bag that had been missing from the table. Now I'm wondering if I took the wrong mental picture. I went into my pocket and fished out my Bic lighter and flicked my Bic. The barrel of a Sig Beretta was pointing at me and pressed up against the bridge of my nose.

"State yo' name varmint, you on my Gillmo's property!" The voice behind the gun stated. I kind of knew who it was when the money from the table was missing. Shannon was my only suspect. He's scandalous like that but he wasn't going to share.

"Shannon, is that your crazy ass?"

"You know it," Shannon stated from the floor on his belly.

"Get your snake slithering ass off the damn floor and let's wrap that shit up and get out of here! You must have been thinking what I was thinking, huh?" I whispered to Shannon as we got off the floor. We couldn't see each other once I put my lighter out.

"Hell yeah, I thought it then my mind was already made up. I had to come back and get this paper and that work. That shit we planned sounded real gangster when we made the commitment but after I thought about it and actually saw the amount of money we were leaving on the table, I said, *fuck that shit I'm going back*," Shannon whispered back to me. I heard a noise coming from the window on the side of the house. That wouldn't be a wise spot to enter, so we knew it wasn't one of our homies. I whispered to Shannon even softer as I raised my showstopper, "Sshh. Somebody is coming."

The light of the moon was coming from the window and then it went black. The image moved slightly and we saw the silhouette of a big round woman booty. We didn't need anymore light to know who it was. "Soncho! What the fuck you doing?" Shannon whispered and startled him a little bit.

He whispered back, "The same as you fools! We came back to get that work. Hey Dante, I told you that nigga Shannon was going to beat us here with his scandalous ass. That was too much paper on the table." Dante was smart and came in through the back window like the rest of us. We couldn't see him but we felt his presence.

"What up, homies? I see Mafia discipline is not in our blood. This is LA. We do shit different."

Grrrrrr!

"What the fuck was that?" Sounds like something growled or gargled.

"I don't like that shit," I heard Soncho whisper.

"Ssshhh, be quiet…" It was real quiet for about 20 seconds. Then we heard it again but it was faint.

Grrrrr.

"You heard that? " Dante asked in the dark.

"Yeah, fool. I don't think that nigga is dead."

"That fool got two in his forehead and his eyes is wide open when we left. He's done," I said before any superstitions started coming into play in that dark room.

"Listen, he ain't dead yet. It sounds like he's still breathing."

"It must be a puppy," Shannon blurted. "They didn't have a dog, did they?"

"That sounds like a human moaning. So go check to see if that fool is breathing," I suggested to anyone that was willing. Soncho pulled out his gun and cocked it.

"Don't shoot him with that 4-5 fool. You going to wake up the whole neighborhood at 3 in the morning. Think about what you're doing. Put one of those throw pillows from the couch over his nose or something," Shannon told him."

"You do that shit!" Soncho thought about it and that throw pillow idea made him uncomfortable.

"What I know you ain't scared now?" Shannon asked sounding nervous himself.

Soncho answered. "Not one bit, but I did enough already. I don't even hear anything now. It was probably the wind."

"Does everybody have a lighter?" I whispered loudly. Everybody took their lighters out so we could see. Dante, Soncho, and I flicked our lighters and looked at Shannon to take the next step.

Shannon got pissed and snatched the pillow off the couch. He directed his anger toward Soncho.

"How are you going to be Scary and Chubby? I'll do that shit my damn self!" Shannon stormed toward the corpse that was half breathing with the pillow gripped tight in his hand. We followed him with our lighters. We looked at Kenyan and he had already started turning a little dark. He didn't look alive but the breathing sound was definitely coming from his area. Shannon lifted the pillow and that dead body leapt up out that chair and jumped on to Shannon, and I thought we were all going to faint.

We weren't prepared for nothing like that to happen. We wanted to help our friend but the state of shock delayed everything. It scared the dog shit out of me! I couldn't even imagine how Shannon was feeling. The look on his face was a mixture of embarrassment, being terrified, and pissed the fuck off 'cause he did not like being the blunt of the practical joke.

Dez's sick ass had Kenyan on his lap and just tossed him up on Shannon. Dez couldn't contain his laughter. Shannon didn't find nothing funny about that joke.

"Hey now motherfucka! Don't be doing that shit, man! You ain't supposed to be playing like that! Don't be tossing no muthafuckin dead niggas on me, man! I don't play them kind of jokes, muthafucka, with no dead ass muthafuckas! I was about to kill that muthafucka!" Shannon kept cussing and trying to get his balls from out being stuck in his stomach.

Dez was cracking up laughing so hard he couldn't even talk. The looks on our scared faces must have been the delight of his life. I've never heard Dez laugh like that before ever. He was always serious, even at the Comedy Act Theater. Dez was going to get whoever came close to the body but I know he was glad it was Shannon. They always had a little rivalry from the days on the playground. By now we were starting to come down to earth and cracking up, too. Shannon was the only one still not laughing but after his heart came back in his body, he had to laugh, too. Dez got us good. Oh Black muthafucka. We scooped up those goods and got the hell up out of there. We were not supposed to be having that much fun at a heinous murder scene.

Chapter 22

"HEY! I'M HAVING A BABY! I'm going to be a Pappy!" Soncho said proud and happy as he walked across the grass with both arms stretched out with the elbows slightly bent. He had a big grin on his face and that little twinkle in his eye. We were having our annual Westside Picnic at Cheviot Hills Park. We all congratulated Soncho and gave him dap after hearing the good news.

"What? I didn't even know you was fuckin' yet!" Shannon clowned Soncho as he gave him a tight hug around the neck. One of the old homies named Screw gave Soncho a terrible sentimental speech. He had already been drinking so it was going to start getting emotional sooner or later.

The picnic was poppin'. Most of the in-crowd that lived or went to school on the Westside of LaBrea was present. It wasn't too crowded but the right mix of people was there. It was a couple of different sets on the premises but we would never have reason to get into conflict with them. We all grew up together pretty much and our relationship was built on that so we left it pure.

DJ Mark Luv was spinnin', and he was so damn cool on a personal level. This brother was so well spoken and the seriousness in his voice infliction actually inspired me to do more for the hood than I have been. DJ Mark Luv wasn't some old Negro preaching White Jesus sermons; he was just like me except for the fact he saw the big picture when it came to unity. We are a self-contained unit and Dez didn't trust anybody, and he was a strong influence on us so it was hard for me to grasp that concept of unity as well but DJ Mark Luv had my attention when he spoke on it.

Bringing it back to the present, he had the park rockin'. All the pretty ladies were in there in Camp Beverly Hills or Flip shirts, fly Bermuda shorts, and fresh sneakers. They were out on the grass dancing, doing *The Guess* and this new dance called *The Snake!* The Snake was already being done at the Ultra Wave dances and on Soul Train but after Janet Jackson did the dance in her new video *"What have you done for me..."* it blew up.

We had a few hood chefs commandeering the grills out there. The Homie Kenny from Hami High was forcing us to eat his BBQ but he was one of those cats that the more he drank, the more shit he added to the meat. He stood over the grill marinating his meat in Old English 800, ketchup, wine coolers, and anything else in his reach. That meat was so dry and burnt we had to work hard to find some tender meat to eat. The homie C-Boy had his BBQ truck out there and it was the best by far. There was food, weed, and drink in abundance but it dissipated within a few hours. We demolished that food. We laughed so hard, we started crying. Having the munchies is a muthafucka. We saw Khan wiping the sauce from the inside of the pan with the end piece of the bread, then he folded it and made a sandwich. That gin he loved so much kept kicking in harder every hour and he needed to come down. All the girlfriends that bought food were bitching 'cause they didn't get a chance to eat their own dishes. And they knew exactly which broads had too much on their plates and which ones came for seconds.

I wouldn't call this day a celebration, but I had to reflect on our early success because we were rollin' on a cool level. We couldn't compete with the Big Dawgs yet but we were doing better than the gang bangin' prototypes. I guess you could say we were Middle Class living Gangsters to be politically correct. In our world, it's about the Strong and the Weak and you don't want to get caught in middle of that shit.

We had the pool hall up for over half the year now, and it was doing what I envisioned. We may have not been maximizing our profits from the actual billiards joint, but it was the best looking, most upscale Pool Hall cats had ever seen. We had laid it out. We had the best felt, called worsted billiard fabric, on the Pool Tables. It was the shit they only used in professional tournaments. Our tables brought the best pool sharks out to play on it. High stakes gambling was evident. We had the best McDermott 19-ounce Pool Sticks. I don't even want to go into the premium chalk we had.

Our bar profits were decent. We had liquor but we didn't go through the proper channels in obtaining the license that expired when we changed ownership. Technically, we were only supposed to have Beer and Wine so we were risking our future doing business like that. We were going to have to fatten some pockets to expedite that liquor license like yesterday, but we didn't know who to reach out to. We were going to figure it out though. We were going to have to venture into another aspect of the game. If you thought street niggas was ruthless they ain't nothing compared to those white-collar criminals. They will purge you of everything and keep you alive to suffer.

But overall, we were living for some 19- and 20-year-old young men that were into all kinds of shit. We hadn't seen any new enemies *as a whole* on the horizon since we cut those Palm Tree Boys down. Shannon kept somebody we never heard of on his heels looking to peel his cap for a reason only Shannon and the potential shooter knew about. We didn't like that shit and Shannon always pretended he had no idea who wanted him. Maybe he didn't. We will never know with Shannon. Whatever he was doing worked for him but what he was into most times, we would never have a clue.

We typically drove Corvettes, Z's, and Porsches, but when we go on one, that's when we would break out the Impala Low Riders and Cadillacs and start wearing French braids and plats. We ain't nothing nice when we're in that mode. Today, we are at peace and looking nice in bright, happy colors.

"Hey Trav, I never told you this, and listen I ain't no punk, this ain't no sissy shit but I love you man. I love you, Trav. If you ever need anything, just ask OG Screw! You hear me? Listen, I'm talking real now. I only came over here to tell you I love you but it ain't no Punk shit. A man can tell a man he loves them, that don't mean we boyfriends or no punk shit fuck that shit… what was I saying? I'm a little drunk… I'm a little drunk and I ain't going to hold you up from all the pretty girls I just want to tell you something… I just came over here to say that," as he stumbled over towards Soncho.

"You love me. I got you, Screw. I love you, too," Soncho said and nudged Screw's drunk ass away from the area.

"Oh, I told you that already?" Screw said and walked over to Dez to tell him the same. That wasn't a good move. Dez doesn't respect OGs that have the *OG* title only for being old and not because of what they did for the game. Dez just socked him and laid him out with a one-shot whammy when Screw opened his arms and tried to hug him.

I shook my head. I felt no sympathy for him. He had fucked up my daydream. Soncho walked over to where I was and pointed to the dude on roller skates in the parking lot with a Boom Box on his shoulder. I looked to where Soncho was pointing and saw the tall, thin roller skater in the flare leg slacks with no pockets in the back and no belt, the tight mid-drift T-shirt with the sleeves cut off and showing his stomach, he was wearing wristbands with a headband that didn't match them. He was skating backwards, and crisscrossing, and doing the crazy noodle leg.

"That muthafucka is everywhere, ain't he? Venice Beach, Ladera Park, LA Coliseum. We've been seeing that fool around for years and I've never seen him walking with regular shoes on," Soncho observed and laughed.

"Congrats again to you and Lu-Lu on your baby coming. You better start putting some money away for the future."

"Oh, here you go now. I live by the day, Trav. Every time I try to save, something goes wrong. I don't have that kind of luck for some reason. I have to get it and spend it or it ends up going someplace else beside the safe, like bills. I don't understand it myself," Soncho confessed.

"Well maybe since you are doing it for your baby on the way, it might have purpose. Try it one more time and if it doesn't work keeping searching until you find a method that sticks. Just don't give up."

"I hear ya. When are you and Toni going to have one so we can bring our kids up together?" Soncho asked like a proud future Pappy.

"Don't put that out there. I am not ready yet. But if it happens, I'm cool with it. I wouldn't ask Toni to have an abortion."

"You love Toni, huh?" Soncho asked.

I thought about it before I answered. "I believe I do. We have a cool fit but she's kind of crazy." I had to let him know it was peaches & beans sometimes, not always cream.

"Well shit, all of them are a little crazy!" Soncho said it like it was something the world didn't know already.

"She came up in the game. I think Toni and her pops was hustling on some confidence shit. She's nothing like her mama. She's a daddy's girl in a real way."

"Speaking of Moms, what going on with Shannon and his mama. He gets an attitude every time her name comes up. Even when we found that stash you said would be in the pool hall and we used it to buy our parents some houses, Shannon was still mad and it was *his* idea. You didn't look too happy, either but you wasn't trippin' like him. That nigga was the one that said, 'Let's just use this free money so we can get our mamas a house.' And then he flipped out. I heard he got her and Pops a nice house out in the furthest part of Lancaster and he's never been in it one time. Is that true?"

"Ain't no telling what goes on in the mind of a Shannon. You don't know that by now? That dude is special," I informed him.

"I feel for him, though. Khan said their mama has been complaining ever since she moved, saying it was too far and her friends don't want to come visit her out that far. She said Shannon only moved her out there to get her away from him. That sounds about right knowing that crazy fool." Soncho pretty much hit the nail on the coffin without me saying if he was right or wrong.

I moved my mama out to the Valley. It was smaller, more expensive, and she had a mortgage to go with her house but she was still close to the civilization she was used to. Despite what happened with that money in the safe, we still had to do our part as children in this game. We dreamed of buying our mamas a house when we hit a certain number. Our dream came true. We were pissed like a muthafucka at first but our parents didn't know any better so I let that shit go. That was the generation they came up in. *Mama and Daddy are always right*.

With that being true or not, we still had to do our part and be successful walking through the doors they opened for us. Shannon was getting purged from Day 1, so he was always irritated by his mama's actions. Pops was Pops and he didn't steal from his son, but he didn't stop his wife from doing it either. But shit, we did a little stealing and killing to get the money in the first place, so who are we to judge? If someone had asked me, it was better having my loved ones hit my safe than an enemy. No. Wait. If an enemy putting a lick on my money, that's part of the game; division in the family over money fucks up the game.

To me personally, Soncho got the worst deal of us all. He brought his mama the cash for her house and she gave the bag to the Church. Now she got the nerve to ask him for money every month for rent 'cause she's behind on her bills from paying tithes. She's still in her apartment in Playboy Hood. She didn't even turn the money in 'cause it was the *devil's money*. No, she gave it to the Church because Jesus spoke to her in a dream. He said, *Juanita, wake up, it's me Jesus.*

Give that money to the Church and feed your people and you'll never have to pay another bill in life again. She had heard those words but it wasn't Jesus. It was Pastor Earl, whispering in her ear after they had one too many glasses of church wine and found themselves in an act of fornication. We weren't surprised because she had been a Holy Roller all her life but now it was becoming too extreme. Soncho told his mama Jesus was Black and their relationship turned just as bad as Shannon and his mama's. If it ain't White Jesus, she did not want it. First, she had him prove it because her Bible makes no mistakes. When he showed her the verse in Revelations, she said she don't care what the Bible says, Jesus and the angels were white and she's going to a White Heaven. Soncho was more embarrassed by his situation 'cause it made his mama look less intelligent.

"But yeah, Soncho, I know we are still young and have a lot of learning to do the hard way so I'm not trying to bombard you with extra pressure or anything, but according to statistics, we have six years or less to live like this so we might want to start thinking of getting your house in order for your baby. I'm just suggesting."

"What are you talking about? That dead or in jail by the time we are 25 bullshit? You are the main one always talking about *we need to break that cycle.* Take your own advice. That is not a future. And you know I'm not talking like we are invincible and that won't happen to me shit. Soon as I would start thinking that way would be the day I got shot. I'm talking about playing the game right like the Elder Pico Nikko was saying. See y'all don't think a fat nigga be listening just 'cause I like snacks, but my ears and eyes are always open."

"I never doubted that once you gave that full commitment to that Westside way of life.

"I'm all in. Here comes Dez and Suge strolling over here. We were thinking about going skating at Flippers or in Reseda and talk some drag to some new ladies. You know those chicks in the hood bounce from member to member until they settle on the one that does it for them. Dante's woman has been with me, you, Shannon, Khan, and one of the little homies, and not on hoe shit. She was our legit girlfriend but we can't pretend like she's somebody we never seen naked before. Doesn't it seem awkward to you sometime?"

"Well, not with her because the pussy wasn't that good," I said truthfully.

""Yeah it was dry and inconsistent. It wasn't good as I thought either. Dante is cool with it and I'm happy for him," Soncho switched his sentiments and smiled out towards the blue skies.

"Yeah, me, too. They make a nice couple." I smiled right along with Soncho.

"What the fuck y'all doing over here smiling at sun like you're in love," Dante laughed as he caught us in our moment of reflection. "That must be some good weed y'all smoking to be smiling like that. Let me hit something."

"You got some rolling papers?" Soncho asked

"I got Papers and a Roller... oh, and a lighter, too."

"But no weed. What kind of nigga is you? You gon' kick in on this sack? Put in ten or you ain't hittin' my weed. You're a freeloader. And I know you got money."

"Man, my money is tied up, you know that," Dante lied as always. My crew keeps money but we lie to each other about how broke we are all the time. Don't ask why we did it. It wasn't on purpose. It was just something in our DNA or our West Coast culture that made us do it.

"Yeah I bet... Tied up in rubber bands in a safe somewhere so you can get that new Porsche. Put in that ten," I interjected and we laughed.

"Man, I can't believe y'all gonna a make me spend my last ten just to hit a joint. Man here, take my last... can I give you just eight so I can at least have two dollars for gas to get home?"

We ignored that fool and started talking to the rest of the homies that walked over. Dez had a bottle of Champagne in an ice bucket. It made the 40-ounce of Mickeys wrapped in the paper bag Khan was sipping on look cheap as hell. Dez's lady walked up behind him and brought us real crystal Champagne glasses. Khan looked at the bottle in his hand and tossed it in the garbage pail.

"Where the hell is Shannon?" Dante asked the question he already knew the answer to.

"Do you even have to ask?" Suge answered and shook his head.

"With who's broad?" I asked and laughed. Dez answered like he was disgusted by Shannon's actions. Shannon was just holding up the toast, and Dez didn't have patience for nonsense.

"OG Screw's old broad is sucking his dick behind that tree over there."

"Screw? The nigga you knocked out over there? Damn you and Shannon sure know how kick a hard-luck nigga when he's down," Soncho spoke out of emotion and didn't truly realize that it made excellent sense. We thought about it and fell out laughing. Shannon came from behind the tree with his pants and draws around his ankles. He walked halfway across the park before he actually pulled his chonies and Polo Shorts up over his bare ass. Half the people in the park saw his black ass out. Shannon did that shit on purpose and it was always a method behind his madness. He claimed the air was knocking the wrinkles out of his shorts as he walked and if we knew anything about quality material, we would know that. Ain't that some shit?

Dez looked at Shannon sideways for holding us up and quickly switched to G mode. He filled our glasses up. We held up our glasses high until they touched in the middle. Dez said, "A Toast to the Westside's Gangster's starting team. This is the nucleus to our set right here. We've already been through enough in this game to let anything come between this tribe. We passed the test of bitches, money, and disloyalty and everything else that brings animosity in the set. Everything we do from this moment forward has to be for a purpose. We are still going to have a lot fun while we're young but when it comes to this level gangster shit we are in now, no games will be played. Due to these so-called OGs like Screw's dumb ass with no knowledge to pass down, we have to learn while we live. Now I want to make a toast to Soncho for being the first one of the homies having a baby. Do the right thing, Big Boy. I also want to make one last toast to Shannon and Trav for buying y'all mamas some houses. I envy that. Some of us don't have that luxury. No matter the circumstances, y'all did that shit. I love y'all. Westside Gangster for Life!"

"Westside!"

"G'd Up!"

We all took a sip and gave each other drunken hugs. We started talking about the normal young gangster picnic shit, money and bitches and how much we were going to spend and get and how many bitches we would have. We were having a ball but in this game you never know when shit is about to jump off. Our guards were all the way down. We were at a Family picnic.

"Hey, who are those fools creeping up over there?" Khan asked nonchalant but his body language was showing that he was getting on point.

I was facing Soncho and my back was turned to what Khan was referring to. I saw Soncho's terrified eyes open wide as silver dollars and before he could finish saying, *"Look Out!"* We all got hit.

Pop-pop-pop-pop!

Ten or fifteen water balloons came raining down on us from all directions like a hailstorm. Our ladies and little cousins and their little friends and play cousins was launching those bad boys at will and lighting our asses up. "Ahhhhhhh shit! Not my new Polo shirt?" Shannon yelled playfully pissed and took off running towards the laughing kids being chased. Soon as Shannon got near these trees, five teenagers jumped out from behind them with super soakers.

They tore Shannon up. He retreated immediately. I chased two boys down and tackled both of them. I robbed them for their water balloon stash. It was on now. Soncho jacked one the little boys for his super soaker and evened this war up. We were having so much pure fun that moment we realized that getting money, luxury cars, having a ménage a trois with beautiful exotic women that like cocaine and gave head so good it could make you change your religious beliefs couldn't be compared. It was just a different kind of pure fun.

Chapter 28

MRS. CHARLENE SUGARS LOOKED shamelessly decadent and dazzling in her blue Valentino evening dress embellished with shimmering crystals in a myriad of geometric patterns that was timelessly fabulous. It had a moderate yet tasteful slit at the front that provided a small hint of sexiness. Mrs. Sugars' jewelry was stunning. It kind of made you step back and glance again without trying to stare too much. She wore a Van Cleef & Arpels cushion-cut diamond and sapphire necklace with the earrings and bracelet to match. Her flawless diamond wedding ring was a Harry Winston design.

Yeah, Mr. Sugars cherished his Goddess as he called her when he was on Earth. He didn't buy her expensive gifts because he had it like that. Mr. Sugars worked hard for his and Mrs. Sugars earned it. She did the same for him. He got everything he wanted and needed. It wasn't one-sided. They were a team. It was a beautiful union. They had an incredible sex life. They spoiled each other when they were up and nursed each other back to health when they were feeling down. Mr. Sugars attended all his wife's political functions, baby showers, friend's weddings, anniversary parties, romantic getaways, and she got all the things women dreamed of doing and desired because she fulfilled all his sexual desires all the time and she knew how to sit down while the football game was on and shut the fuck up. You can't get a woman better than that. He didn't want much but some good lovin' and peace of mind. He bought a nice house, had good family, money in the bank, and most of his goals in life were met, it was time to live. Mr. Sugars was old school with young ideas. It was tragic his life was cut so short.

Suge was upset that he had to attend the gala affair with his mother on last minute notice. Mrs. Sugars' escort had to stay in Washington, DC, on important business. Suge usually didn't mind going with his mother like he's done many times in the past, but he was older now and did not like the way the rented tuxedo fit him. The pants were bell-bottom, the shoes were Bozo, the cummerbund and that snap-on bow tie that came with it was not happening. It looked more like a cheap-ass prom suit than fly dinner wear. It was all about styling. But right then, Suge couldn't find a dinner jacket to save his soul. He called up one of his homies that banged with those trendy gangs from K.O.D. that turned the Ultra Wave parties out and learned how to taper his tuxedo pants. He refused to wear bell-bottom slacks with his prom hook up. The suit knocked three years off of Suge and made him look 16 again.

Suge was also perturbed because Dante wasn't attending the function. Dante moved that soft powder to those politicians and it was always profitable. In that political circle, the façade was Suge was the model student and Dante was the spoiled rich prep school kid from a single parent home that was intelligent but defiant. He stayed with the Sugars from time to time to keep out of trouble. It was far from the truth but that's how they played it for the past few years. A few of the politicians had rebellious private school kids like that themselves so they had a soft spot for Dante. Suge couldn't risk putting the image he established on the line for a few dollars. That was bad for business and they would start looking at Mrs. Sugars differently from then on. Without Dante, the soiree was just going to be another boring dinner party with his mother as his date.

"Things seem to be going well with that pool hall? I didn't know you could make as much money as I see you with from people playing pool all day. I hope you are not into selling those drugs I hear about on TV and at work," Mrs. Sugars quizzed her son.

"You know I used that money Dad left me to go in on that business, Mom. Stop letting those politicians at your job fill your head with stories. They are the biggest crooks. You know that. We are going to a fundraiser full of felons that never get caught right now. Overall business is good, but we might lose it."

"Already? Are you behind on rent? I'll loan you the money if it's not too much."

"No, it's not that. We need a liquor license. That's where we make our money."

"Are you sure that's how you get money for Porsche cars and Corvettes? Selling liquor? Now, I heard stories about Shannon and Dez. Please be careful, son."

"You know I am, Mom."

"I really miss your father in times like these. He would know what to say to you. I just sound like a mother."

"Well you sound good. Don't worry so much. You did a great job. If I were to get into anything—and that's *if*—hypothetically speaking, it would be on me, and not a negative reflection of you. I'm a big man now."

"OK. I'm going to take your word for it." Mrs. Sugars paused. "By the way, I think Assemblyman Shareece Wright can help you get that liquor license. You will probably have to make a small contribution to one of his *many funds* but I'm quite sure he can do it with no problem. I've seen them do it for friends and relatives opening bars all the time."

"We would sure appreciate that. I hope he won't want some astronomical figure because we are underage. Those politicians are crooks. I don't trust them but we need any help we can get at this point."

"Like you said, he's crooked. If the price is right, he won't care if you're twelve years old."

"Hey. I didn't tell you yet, Mom, but you look absolutely beautiful.

It actually feels kind of weird having my mom take my breath away. Wow! I need friends like Shannon and Dez to keep the wolves off of you tonight."

"Oh cut that out, boy! You are making your Mother blush. You have that same charm just like your Father. Boy, I do miss him."

"I miss Pop, too… everyday."

$$ \$ \ \$ \ \$ \ \$ \ \$ $$

Shannon, Dez, Soncho, and I met up with Chris and his white homeboy Brandon at Ed Debevic's Restaurant at the foot of Beverly Hills. It was a 50's retro diner. We liked going there 'cause we felt like this is what the show *Happy Days* would look like if they had Black people on there. The little intricate details in décor, the beehive hairstyles and horn-rimmed glasses on their waitresses, and the steady merriment of lip-synced 1950 dance numbers were cute. We ordered a basket of Cheese Fries, Burgers, and Cherry Sodas.

"What's on your mind, homeboy? What you got for us?" Shannon asked. Dez kept his eyes on Brandon. He was studying what kind of white man this dude was. A lot of them in the game looked like they had hood ties but when the pressure was on them they turn back lily white and leave the nigga to take the fall.

"My man Brandon here is a certified Fiber Optic Technician that specializes in installing cable television and most importantly home security systems. Did I mention that he works out in the Bel Air and Beverly Hills area? Brandon is being overwhelmed by new customers and is looking to hire some well-bodied and intelligent employees that fit the job description. I'm just here to give a reference. Brandon can tell you more about it," Chris passed the baton as he concluded after the briefing.

"The jobs split evenly between us usually average around ten to twenty dollars an hour. Some jobs pay a lot more but never anything less than what I mentioned or I won't do it. It's not worth all the work that goes into it. I need a team that's tough mentally -and physically if need be but that should never be the case. I run a professional operation. I don't give orders but I expect you to follow the plan I bring to the table exactly the way it's laid out. Let's be clear, it has nothing to do with calling shots but everything to do with keeping us out of jail and getting paid good money. Is this a job you may be interested in?"

Ten to twenty thousand dollars a piece minimum to do a house move in Bel Air with a cool ass white boy with all the alarm codes, and a fence to dump the merchandise sounded good to me.

"I'm down. Count me all in," I said without hesitation but not seeming eager at all.

"I'm in."

"I'm down, too."

"I just hope I don't have to climb up on nothing high. You know I don't like being on roofs and shit," Soncho spoke out inappropriately. We would worry about his weight loss and fear of heights later. Brandon looked at us to see if we had any weaknesses that he should know about We ignored Soncho like he didn't even speak and continued with business.

"Do you have any job assignments contracted for us or is this *just to feel us out* meeting?" Dez asked. He beat me to my question. Brandon reached into his back pocket and had a simple diagram of a house, the entrance points, blind spots, hot spots, times to hit the lick, alarm codes, and schematics. We were wishing Khan were there. As terrible as he is in school, he was crafty with electronics from watching the educational channels. Shannon and Khan always watched shows we considered weird since we were little. Shannon loved MASH and old programs white people watch on CBS, Channel 2. Khan would find programs on the UHF channels. When we were little they had a TV with two dials. The one up top was for Channels 2-13. The Bottom one was for Channels 14-60. Khan stayed on those channels watching Wood Shop and Inventions programs.

We checked out what he had and agreed on the terms. We ordered another round of Cherry 7-Ups. We poured half out into our empty water glasses. Since business was over, Shannon pulled out a pint of IW Harper Whiskey and refilled our glasses. We stirred them up until it was nice and blended and made a toast to a profitable and successful lick.

$ $ $ $ $

"Yes, you're turning into a fine young man. Have you considered what college you may be attending in a couple of years? It may seem like years away but it comes faster than you can blink your eye! Ha ha ha ha!" Congressman Maynard laughed at his corny jokes while he kept patting Suge on the back and squeezing his shoulder every other word. Everybody always seems to think Suge was only 16.

"I was considering USC and Howard University."

"Stick with USC. You don't want to mess around with those all black nigger schools. My father told me they weren't worth the price of the bus ticket it takes to get there. White schools are the way to go," Congressman Maynard said as he patted Suge continuously on his back.

Suge thought that was the worst advice he ever heard. He missed his father terribly in that instant. *My father would never say some dumb shit like that*, Suge thought, and he moved away from him to the next politician after the next, with the same what seemed like scripted conversation. Suge shook the hands and brown-nosed fifty old-ass politicians at the Biltmore Hotel in downtown Los Angeles and not one of them was Shareece Wright. But in between the old politicians, Suge entertained himself and kissed the hands of the women, flashing his beautiful smile.

Once the free drinks kicked in, all the stiff political wives and widows wanted to be kissed somewhere… on something. Suge didn't have to be overprotective of his mother because she carried herself the way she looked, elegant. Even in death, the respect for Mr. Sugars still hovered over certain men that may have felt his seriousness about his goddess in years past. The gentlemen that asked Mrs. Sugars for a dance without acknowledging Suge first were not allowed to. Suge took it as extreme disrespect, especially with his mother's arm clasped around his. Suge would forcefully move their hand when they held it out to Mrs. Sugars and politely tell them she wasn't interested. The gentlemen that asked Suge were granted the permission to have his mom's hand for a dance.

Suge walked over to the punch bowl. There was a young 14-year-old white girl pouring herself a glass. She looked like she was sneaking it. Suge assumed she thought it was liquor in it. She looked at Suge and creamed her panties. She didn't see many black guys where she lived so anything taboo turned her on. Suge could have been Mexican and it wouldn't have mattered as long as it was something her parents despised. She was bad, and not bad meaning good. She was devious and manipulating. Suge knew she was a case waiting to happen.

She went to an all-girl boarding school to keep her away from city life. She offered Suge her glass and poured herself another. Suge thanked her and took a sip. The punch did have liquor in it and Sun Daniels—that was her name—had poured it in there. She was tickled pink like she just pulled off a great caper.

Suge chatted with her for a little while, but she was too young and silly for him. She was a bit too promiscuous, too. She kept moving her lollipop around in her mouth signaling she wanted to give him a blowjob, but Suge declined to act on her signals. Shannon would have loved to have that moment.

The only mistake Suge made was making friends with her. He was bored and she was at least close to his age. She followed him around every chance she got. Suge wasn't seasoned enough to know how to keep that rich freak around for another four years and cash in when she turned 18. At that moment, she was a pest and any amount of money wasn't worth it. Sun wasn't a looker but she was catching the eye of a dirty old horny Assemblyman named Shareece Wright. Suge didn't know who he was at the time, but he saw Mr. Wright's eyes looking at Sun's long legs with lust in his eyes.

Suge cut in on his mother's dance partner without asking to get Sun away from him. She was on her fifth glass of the spiked punch in that many minutes and was becoming unbearably goofy and trying to entice her dance partner out in to the parking lot of the Biltmore Hotel. After more fake smiles, handshakes, and three boring speeches, Suge was finally introduced to Assemblyman Shareece Wright. Suge didn't know how to take it but it seems like he was just as eager to meet him. Shareece made small talk grand and boasted how great his mother was to the community and doesn't get the credit she deserves and all that jazz. Then he excused himself from Mrs. Sugars and asked if he could talk to Suge in private.

Assemblyman Shareece Wright was nothing special. He stood over 6 feet and was stout from being able to eat well everyday but far from obese. He was the typical brown skinned, cheese eatin' Negro that stuck his chest out around Black People that thought he was somebody and kept his tail between his legs and changed his voice when Whitey was around. He was married to a stiff haired petite woman with big lips and not the dick sucking kind and she had wide coffee stained teeth. She dressed liked a White President's wife and always wore pearls. He had a couple of funny looking kids that will eventually follow in their Daddy's political footsteps. They already looked the part.

"So Soog, your mother—"

"Suge, my name is pronounced Suge," He corrected him politely.

The congressman smiled as if he didn't realize his mistake. "Right.

So Suge, your mother was telling me you would like to make a nice contribution to my Fight Student Illiteracy fund. She also told me you might need a little help in obtaining a certain permit to keep your business operations going." He paused for a moment. "Now there are some people that say it's not good to go into business with friends, but I don't believe that. I like doing business with friends. It's more up close and personal. There is a sense of guilt that comes with crossing a friend in business that you have to live with for the rest of your life. I want to be friends and not just business associates. I screen my friends carefully to make sure they are who they portray themselves to be. I asked a few of my colleagues here whose names will remain anonymous in this conversation that say you are very, very cool, Suge. Is that true? Are you cool?"

"Like the other side of the pillow," Suge answered smooth and not too arrogant. The anonymous ones Shareece Wright was refereeing to were the congressman tat Dante sold nose candy to. Suge didn't know if that was a good thing. They already broke the confidentiality agreement by letting Shareece Wright know he was "Cool." That was not cool. That was their business and the less people knew about it, the cooler everyone could all remain. Nevertheless, he knew Suge could make things happen comfortably. Suge was hoping he didn't want any cocaine or pills because he didn't come prepared.

"I might be able to help you out. I can talk to a few of my people I know downtown and pull a few strings. I might even be able to waive the financial contribution if you are willing to pay in other ways... oh, by the way, what happened to your little girlfriend? You can share the good news," Shareece Wright asked in a devilish tone. Suge was quickly about to dismiss that notion and for some reason the words couldn't come out. He decided to play it out.

"She's around here somewhere trying to avoid her parents. She had a few glasses of that spiked punch over there and she's more than a little tipsy."

"How close are you to her?" Assemblyman Wright just put it out there.

"How close am I to getting that liquor license in my hands?"

CHAPTER 24

"G'S UP!" I answered the phone around 2am. I was still up watching a movie with Toni.

"What up homie, I have great news!" Suge cheered like the words were tickling his tonsils as he spoke. Christiane was massaging his shoulders and relaxing him from being around all those stiff politicians telling shitty jokes all night.

"I can hear it in your voice. You must have came up on a nice lick."

"Naw, naw, nothing like that but I got that liquor license on lock, homeboy! And it didn't cost as much as we thought. I pretty much got it for free I just threw a couple of hundred dollars in his fund anyway, just on some Player shit, you know how we do it."

"What else did you do? Slide him some of that good white Peruvian blow?" I asked, being familiar with the stories Suge and Dante shared with us about what goes on low key in those political parties in the past.

"You know that's Dante's hustle at those parties. I have to play the square to keep my mother's image immaculate. I slid him a different kind of white though. The Black Man's other Kryptonite—"

"A White Woman!"

"Yes Sir, but not quite. Mr. Wright is one of those old freaky ass niggas and he had me spit some drag to get this goofy 14-year-old white girl that was drunk off of spiked fruit punch to show him her freckled titties and flash her cat a couple of times while he watched her and jacked off. Sun thought he was creepy but—"

Click.

"Hello?"

Christiane wasn't intending on ear hustling in on Suge's and my conversation even though she was standing right behind him, but it hit too close to home. She snatched the phone out of his hand and slammed it down. Before Suge could ask her what the fuck was going on, she was already explaining.

"Baby, please tell me you took some pictures."

"What? Pictures? Where in the hell would I get a camera from at a black tie dinner?"

"The media that was there or break-in the gift shop. I don't know. Take some cardboard and make a pinhole camera if you have to! Baby, that was your ticket. Opportunities like that only come once in a lifetime. Baby, if you would have got a photograph of that sick pedophile fuck, he would be at your servitude for the remainder of his life."

"What? You talking about an extortion move?"

"Baby! That was the Golden Ticket. It's better than money. Extortion is just a quick payday that simply goes away. You keep a sick bastard like this in your pocket. Milk them for license and zoning permits like the Gentleman's Club we were looking into, a get out of jail free card, businesses where we can launder money legally, like Churches. The Golden Ticket, baby!" Christiane was so depressed she almost started crying. Suge was feeling bad now, knowing he didn't seize the opportunity

"Damn! I fucked up. I fumbled the ball, dammit! Thanks for that game, I owe you one, Christiane," Suge said, but inside, he was disgusted with his rookie move. He wasn't there to meet Pico Nikko in Chicago and missed a valuable lesson on politician control. I'm more than sure he would have been able to capitalize after the elder's words of wisdom and survival.

"Well, do you think you can get him in that position again?

$ $ $ $ $

"Listen cuz, when we roll up on these fools get to dumpin', drop them niggas, then we gon' stab up out of there! You feel me?" Noopy gave the last minute orders to his homeboys that were PCP'd up, feeling violent and looking for enemies on the Eastside of LA. They had a new recruit, Lil Noopy II with them on his first drive-by shooting. He was scared even with the chemical Phencyclidine courage in his system. He was fidgety and that narcotic was slowly starting to control his actions. OG Noopy's words were the only thing keeping his mental state in the present.

"There goes four of those busters from Graze Avenue right there slippin'," Big Ronnie whispered in the front seat. He got shot in the neck a few years back by some OGs from Graze Avenue so everything he said came out in a whisper.

"Hey cuz, turn off those headlights and turn that muthafuckin' radio down—I said, turn that radio down! Hit the ignition and coast in neutral. We fittna' light these niggas up!" Noopy said as he leaned his upper body out of the back window of the stolen four-door bucket they were rolling in. Lil Noopy sat in the back window with his little .25 rested on the roof of the car. Big Ronnie put his arm out the window and let it hang low with the AK-47 in his hand. The four Crips from Graze Avenue was still slippin' with their backs turned toward the streets.

Slim Crippin' from Graze Avenue was walking across the street to meet his homeboys as Lil Noopy positioned himself in the back window. Big Ronnie leaned his head out and yelled, "What's up now niggas! What that EDG like?"

The first shot that went off was the one to the back of Lil Noopy's head at close range with Slim Crippin' behind the trigger. The force of the gun blast caused Lil Noopy's upper body to whiplash and he fell backwards in the street bloodied on the cold concrete. Big Ronnie and OG Noopy had started dumping and letting loose with those AK-47s; they didn't even know they lost a soldier. Two Crips from Graze heard the first shot go off and was on point. They hit the ground and came back up blasting back at the car. The one that ran was the only one that got shot up real bad. They mowed his ass down like tall grass in the winter. Another one was hit but not enough to slow him down. Slim Crippin kept shooting in the car and caught the driver in both shoulders as the bullets came through the back of the car seat. OG Noopy caught one in the calf but it went in and out on the other side. He took notice to Slim and sprayed his way to back him off the car.

"Start this muthafucka and stab out, cuz!!"

The driver started the car but he was starting to panic. Slim Crippin's last shot went through the driver's chest. He hit the gas and made it two blocks before he began to swerve and smash into park cars. As his life was leaving his body, all of his weight came down on the gas pedal and the car reached the speed of 70mph before it crashed head first into a corner church.

Big Ronnie survived the crash but the injuries he sustained from the windshield breaking in his face and the dash board smashing against his knees prevented him from getting out of there. OG Noopy was shook up but got his shit together enough to get up out of there. Noopy thought his calf was on fire. His run turned into a fast hobble real quick, and after about a hundred yards, it turned into a painful limp. Noopy could hear the police sirens coming, and they were getting closer and closer. It wasn't soon after that the sound of the ghetto bird hovering three blocks over that made his slick getaway a sticky situation. Noopy did not want that helicopter to make visual contact on foot in a residential hood that wasn't his. He might as well give it up, but Noopy hit a backyard and hid in an old storage unit full of spiders, cobwebs, half open bags of fertilizers, and old lawnmowers that haven't been used in years.

More and more police cars were filing in. They had the streets blocked off with yellow tape about a half a mile in radius. The Police took their time putting their investigation together either because they knew what happened from experience or they really didn't give a fuck about a gang related drive-by shooting in South Central LA that didn't involve any innocent civilians caught in the crossfire. If that Church wouldn't have had the front end of a Buick lodged into the side of it enough to 'cause a stir at the local black newspaper, the LA Sentinel, the police would have bagged up the driver and Lil Noopy and been gone. It took just a few seconds for the young rookie detective trying to earn his stripes to spot the blood droppings on the ground heading away from the car smashed into the church. It took even less time than that for the K9 unit to let those German Shepherds loose to go hunt nigga. It was in season. The cops lead them to the droppings and they started sniffing the grounds like lines of cocaine was laced on the concrete. Soon as those dogs smelled it was nigga blood, they started wagging their tails. They took off. The cops could barley keep up with them. They got to the house and the cop unhooked their leashes and ordered, "Go get 'em, boys!"

Those dogs tore into that backyard and started clawing, growling, barking, and scratching at that shed like they were ready to tear Noopy's limbs off. Noopy still had his AK-47. If he shot the dogs and hit the back fence that led to the next yard, he could have been out and got away. Noopy was prepared to shoot it out with the cops but he couldn't shoot the dogs. He was a dog lover. Even if he wasn't, killing the white man's dogs is automatic capital punishment. Shooting those niggas up back there was probation if he played it right. Those vicious K9s didn't seem to have the same affection towards Noopy as he did for them.

Noopy came out of the shed with his hands raised and the police hadn't gotten back there. Noopy still had time to lick off two shots, dead those dogs, and be out. He couldn't do it. Those dogs tore the flesh off the side of his face when they leaped on Noopy and knocked him to the ground. The arm that was holding the AK was mauled so bad it was going to require surgery eventually. Both dogs started pulling him by his jacket across the ground. Noopy was pleading to the cops to get the dogs off of him. The Police cuffed him and that was that… Noopy was done…unless he had something to bargain with.

<h2 style="text-align:center">$ $ $ $ $</h2>

Dez, Shannon, Khan, Brandon, and I met up at Westside Billiards at 3am. We didn't officially change the name yet for fear of losing clientele. Even though we remodeled the joint and made it ten times better than before, the thought of some young Black men being able to pull that off doesn't sit well with a lot of folks. So we kept the Japanese Symbol and Dragon logo and just called it Westside Billiards on the streets. The word spread until it became a brand name. We just told everyone we knew the Japanese lettering said *Westside Billiards*. Nobody spoke Japanese but a few Asian gamblers to challenge it so they thought it was slick. The regular customers thought we were just amateur Pool Players and we kept that façade up.

Under normal circumstances, we would have never met there after doing a lick but we had trust issues with Brandon and him with us. On a personal level, everything was great. As far as business, this was our first job together so we were building up that trust as we worked. Brandon was already skeptical because we insisted on bringing Khan with us. It was only a three or four man job and he wasn't needed. We explained he was just there as an extra lookout and we would take care of his share out of our end. We really brought Khan to learn from Brandon. We were taking him to school so he could step up his electronic game. He shadowed Brandon as we hit this big-ass mansion in Beverly Hills. We could tell that was Brandon's hustle because we went in with specific instructions. We knew exactly what we were coming to get. House moves in the hood are raggedy. Those low-level crooks leave your house a mess. We went in wearing all black and came back with cash and jewels that were easy to obtain and some videotape masters that were locked in the safe that took some serious work. Being square to that hustle, we were extremely disappointed when Brandon finally cracked the safe open and tapes came out instead of cash. We never questioned it, but I saw the air of disappointment escape my homies' bodies. Nevertheless, we did the job and got up out of there.

When we got back and divvied up the cash and jewels 4-ways. We yielded about twelve grand apiece roughly, but the big payoff was going to come later for those master tapes. We hit the house of an illegal smut and child porn producer named Russell Monday that would be willing to pay a hefty sum to buy them back. Russell Monday couldn't even call the police to report the break in. He had a case pending related to sexual misconduct, but I'm not sure what it was because it wasn't our concern. Brandon knew the value of the tapes. That's why he had already negotiated a flat rate for that aspect of the job. The number he threw out there was so good we didn't question if we were getting cheated or not. We shook hands on it. Brandon was about his business. He left us something of value, half the master tapes to hold as a good faith gesture until he got the money from Monday but he said we can rest assured he was coming back for them.

We concluded business and made some drinks.

"You guys mind if a few ladies come through to break the testosterone? I got some friends in Santa Monica near here that want to party. They're white chicks, if that's cool?" Brandon asked, as he got comfortable on the barstool.

"Snow bunnies? They probably have flat asses. Are they sucking dick?" Shannon asked while he held his manhood hoping Brandon said yes. Brandon was kind of uncomfortable with the way Shannon phrased the question. Even though Brandon was thinking it, he would have never said it so harsh. And at the same time, he had to protect his friends from this banshee of horny thugs.

"That's up to you and the girl that likes you," Brandon answered and shifted his seat slightly toward Khan and struck up a conversation with him. Even though the joint was locked up and closed for business, I didn't feel comfortable with cash, stolen goods, and illegal porn masters neatly stacked and divided in the middle of the unoccupied pool table. I took the tapes to the back and secured them in our storage room. Shannon rolled a skinny joint. It was thin but it packed a punch. It wasn't long before the freaks came and joined the party. They were friendly, but they weren't down for an orgy. Their allegiance was to Brandon. A couple of them were girlfriends of his homies. They paid for their drinks even though the bar was technically closed. That was the first signal that let us know they were not there to freeload. They were there to party after-hours. They brought their own cocaine and clove cigarettes. Brandon did two lines of coke with them, but he was more of a bottle of Corona type of dude. Brandon got high from doing licks, skydiving, and buying expensive sports cars. That was his rush. He was an adrenaline junkie. Shannon didn't agree with the terms. He liked head before he went to bed. He made a couple of phone calls but his girls needed rides to Santa Monica and he was already too comfortable to drive across town and back.

Dez came up though. The girl Ingrid from Germany was attracted to Dez's strong but quiet demeanor. Ingrid was intrigued with the pain she saw deep in his eyes, and the lines on the palms of his hands that represented the tough journey he's survived. Ingrid talked with Dez and stroked his palms slowly and real gentle the entire night as if she were easing the pain and letting Dez know the journey wasn't in vain. Ingrid was in awe of Dez more than sexually attracted to him so it seemed. Dez remained serious with Ingrid and never flashed one smile. He liked her conversation and would rather have her for a friend. Their common interests were something else. It truly showed that when color and race is taken out of the equation human beings are lying underneath. They both loved to read Walter Mosley Novels, watching the TV Show *Dallas* and foreign movies with subtitles, they loved paintings by Thellus, Inka One, and Ernie Barnes, and musically they loved The Doors more than anything else.

Ingrid had a live unreleased in the U.S. version of *"When the Music is Over"* she brought with her from Germany. It was on a plain white cassette and Dez turned it up loud. We resisted at first wanting to hear some funk but the song took us to another place. It chilled us the fuck out and we really started vibing. It was the perfect song for the setting. The version had to be at least 45 minutes long. It was getting close to 5:30 in the morning before we realized we had been up a half hour shy of 24 hours. The adrenaline of the lick, liquor, Ty weed, and good conversation came down hard all at the same time. We noticed Khan's head and neck jerking backwards and popping back up trying to fight the sleep kicking his ass. That's when Brandon checked his watch. He was still alert but he was ready for some pancakes and eggs. Some hot French toast was starting to sound kind of good. We went from being sleepy to being hungry as a muthafucka.

"Are we going to The Pancake House or Norms?" I asked.

"What about the Beverly Hills Café? Let's get some of those bomb-ass smothered potatoes, nigga, and some buttermilk pancakes! With that sweet, hot syrup leaking on the sausage, that's the shit!!" Khan suggested as he woke up out of his stupor. He said it with so much passion he had everybody in the joint starving.

"Damn! That shit sounds good. But I got to get to my side of town gentlemen," Brandon declined and picked up his keys.

"Man, the 405 is right there! You'll be in Bel Air in ten minutes," I asked, wondering why Brandon didn't want to eat with us. Brandon kept checking his watch all of a sudden. He was cool and relaxed all night to the early morning, now he seemed to be nervous and in a hurry. I didn't like his energy. He could have been jittery from the cocaine in his system, too. I gave him the benefit of the doubt but my antennas were up.

"Well the Cafe would be out of my way and I'm not doing Norms after what Khan just said. I'm going to this little spot out by my way. I'll hit you guys up in a few hours. Try to get some rest," Brandon was saying while he was making his exit out of the door. His homegirls followed quickly behind him though Ingrid stayed with Dez. He was going to take her home after breakfast.

It took us another 20 to 30 minutes to clean up the joint. "Five to One" was playing until the cassette tape came to the end. It automatically clicked and flipped over to the other side. *"When the Music is Over…"* started playing again. We were going to be gone long before it finished this time. We didn't have another 45 minutes in us no matter how good it sounded.

"Let's put this ugly ass jewelry up and come get this money off the pool table and let's roll. I'm starvin'," Shannon said. We were going to be open for business at noon. There was a faint tap on the door. We weren't tripping because we all heard it. It wasn't a hard knock so we didn't get on the defensive.

Shannon asked, "Did one of y'all lock that door back after Brandon and the chicks left?"

We looked around at each other not knowing if we did. Just as soon as I went to check, the Police came in deep with guns out yelling, "FREEZE! Keep your hands up where we can see them!"

The first thought that popped in our heads were the same words Dez mumbled to us, "We're killing that white boy and that nigga Chris!"

"We're already knowing," Shannon whispered back. Underage in a bar with cash and stolen merchandise on the table wasn't going to prevent us from making bail. At the same time, a Breaking and Entering case shouldn't have even brought these many police but then again, Black dudes doing robberies in Beverly Hills would 'cause a stir. Regardless of the situation, it was obvious Brandon snitched and set us up and we agreed he should be terminated with extreme prejudice.

We all got in the arresting position before the police even told us to turn around. The LAPD has been putting us in it since we were eleven years old. It was natural after nine years of it. Ingrid was scared and wishing she would have left with her friends. One of the officers was Jewish, the mean one that didn't like Germans, and had her terrified.

The police officers saw the money and jewelry on the table and didn't concern themselves with it at all. They were pretending like it wasn't even there. They looked at a picture the Sergeant was holding and one of the officers said, "Yeah, that's him!"

They walked straight over to Dez, stated his first and last name and asked if it was him. When Dez said yes, they turned him around and cuffed him while they read his Miranda Rights. We were all thrown for a loop then. We didn't know what the fuck was going on. We had guns in the pool hall not to mention the fucked up videotapes that would ruin us for life. We didn't know how to play it so we stayed quiet. Ingrid flipped the fuck out and barked at the Jewish officer.

"You think you can just come kidnap people and take them away from their loved ones anytime you want, huh? Just because he's black? This is just more racist American bullshit! Your entire U.S. is full of hypocrites. I'm going to have my parents call their lawyer and get you out right away, Dez!"

"Save your dollars, sweetie. He won't be coming home anytime soon. Use this moment to say a long goodbye," the arresting officer informed us all even though he was speaking directly to Ingrid with a shitty grin on his face.

"Why do you say that? What is the charge?" Ingrid demanded with her chest out.

"Murder, sweetheart… in the first degree."

CHAPTER 25

HOURS UPON HOURS HAD passed before we got any more information. We were still a little spooked not knowing if the police were setting us up by pretending to ignore us but they didn't even ask us our names. That had never happened before. The LAPD would flag us down and ask us our names just for walking to school. We didn't even know what this life was about then. Targeting one individual in a room full of guilty criminals was boggling our young minds.

We all posted up at Suge's mom's house. We needed to be in a nurtured environment, relaxed, and comfortable so we could think clearly. Suge brought Christiane with him. She was a very attentive young lady. She had good vision capable of seeing the bigger picture. Christiane was committed to Suge but she would eventually be a benefit to us all. Suge and Christiane was a couple but not like boyfriend and girlfriend. It was something else going on. These were my best friends forever, but once we got in the game, we all changed. It's hard to explain. I know what my homies do, but I really don't know what they are doing. We do things together but we always have other shit going on separately. We've always been like that. We were in hypothetical mode, drumming up scenarios, possibilities, being very pessimistic, spooking ourselves thinking of the worst, what we should do, and really wondering what the fuck was going on with Dez.

Mrs. Sugars came in from work looking like royalty underneath her political/School Principal-style pants suit. She had been at work all day and was still looking perfect. Not a wrinkle in her suit or a hair out of place. We sat up straight and greeted her like good children should.

Mrs. Sugars saw the worried looks on our faces and immediately said, "Now what's going on here?"

We had to confess what was going on. Mrs. Sugars reacted like a mother would. She was concerned for Dez and naturally she thought of her son being in that situation locked up in a funky ass jail and it made her sad and nauseous. She started crying and went to the kitchen to eat a couple of saltine crackers to settle her stomach. We didn't like seeing her like that. I don't know if those saltine crackers acted as a wonder drug or if Mrs. Sugars overhearing our conversation on the possibilities of how to get Dez out if he makes bail that healed her, but she sure came storming out of the kitchen after hearing Shannon say, "Suge, you think your Mom will put up her house? You know we can't show cash like that."

"I am NOT putting my house up for that nigga. I love Dez like he's my own son but I'm not putting my house up, even for my own son," Mrs. Sugars stated with a stern attitude we had never seen before.

"Mom!"

"What? I'm not stupid, Suge. I don't think you guys are bad kids but I know you're into some bad things. If I put my house up and Dez takes off running like he should if he's knows he can't win, I'm out of a house. Your daddy taught me that. His own mother almost lost her house when his brother jumped bail on her. It was a mess. No, no."

The rest of our parents were out of the question. After the lecture from Mrs. Sugars, we didn't even consider it and we had bought them the houses. They were not going for that. That's the generation they were from. All they had to do was hear a story of about somebody they didn't even know about something that went wrong and that was it. Their mind was made up. Gathering solid facts or learning from their own experiences never applied. I know if my mama left me in jail and wouldn't put up the house to get me out that I bought. I'm burning it down. I would buy her another one but I would be so mad I would have to do something. What we knew about Dez's parents was vague. He had parents but that was the extent of it. We never spent the night at his house when we were little or kicked it over there.

But we had the pool hall and as long as it didn't bring us any heat, we were willing to put it up if we had to.

"Hey Mom, don't you have some of your politician friends that can pull some strings and get our friend out of jail? All that money you help them raise has to mean something?" Suge kind of blurted out just reaching for anything, like hope. He put his face in his hands not even looking for a response to his question.

Mrs. Sugars shook her head at the stupidity of the question. "Yeah, it means I can keep a good job and that's about all it means. That part of politics is a whole different level. Your mama is old school and by the books. I hear of certain politicians, lawyers, and judges pulling strings for each other but I mind my own business and do what they pay me for. I don't want anything to do with that stuff. It's messy."

"Shareece Wright can't help? He helped with the license for the business."

"Ha ha! He probably would want you to believe he could. He wants to run with the sharks. But I guess you can ask him. It wouldn't hurt. "

That was the best hope we heard since Dez got flagged off. For now, it wasn't anything we could do but wait. Dez's lawyer finally contacted us at Mrs. Sugars' home. His name was Leo Cohen. We were taught to believe we would always have a better shot at beating a case if a white lawyer represented us. The things we had to learn along the way to dispel those dumb ass myths were costly. Leo Cohen kept the conversation professional and told us to meet with him in person for a talk at his office in Beverly Hills the following day. Leo also informed us he had Dez on his other line and he would put him on the speakerphone.

"What up homies? G's Up. Y'all good?"

"Better than you OG, what the fuck is going on? You all right?"

"Just some bullshit that can get real serious for your boy in a minute.

I need Trav or Suge or Dante—anybody but Shannon's forgetful *I'm going to take my time* ass—down to Cohen's office on the quick and lay some bread on him. I'm good for it. I just can't get to it right now in these conditions. I'm in a steel box. Get down there on time for your homie and I'll hit you with that intel. Hey, man, be down there, Cohen got shit all arranged already. Time is of the essence. I'm cool though. They put me in the Crip Module 'cuz it's still on my juvenile jacket from some HKK shit back in the day. But you know, it's just niggas; we got to deal with that everyday. You know me, I just don't like choosing no side unless it's Westside. Just handle that business for me. Hey, all the homies is up in here! Big Psycho from Lynwood, Tootle Bear from Watts, I saw OG Left Nut but I didn't get to holler at him. Man, he's still in here fighting that hot one from three years ago."

"Does he still have one nut?" Soncho asked out of curiosity but don't ask why.

"Shit, I guess, nigga. I don't think balls can grow back after you lose one," Dez answered like WTF does it matter. We laughed it off and started asking about other homies that went to county jail at one time or another and have yet to return. Dez ran off a few more names. We started talking about everything but his case. Leo Cohen never interrupted the conversation. We talked until it was time for Dez to check in for head count.

We still didn't have too much information to go on but knowing Dez was safe and we weren't involved took a lot of pressure off of our minds. It was much easier to focus on saving one ass instead of seven.

$ $ $ $ $

The following morning Suge put in a call to Assemblyman Shareece Wright's direct line. Suge wasn't supposed to have that number but he took advantage of the exclusive connections his mother had in her phone book. Assemblyman Wright was a little agitated that Suge called on his private line but then remembered that little favor he did for him at the fundraiser that put a freaky little smile on his face. Assemblyman Wright stayed in character during the brief conversation talking to Suge like he was practicing his campaign speech. Soon as he acknowledged Suge's greeting, Assemblyman Wright immediately asked, "I sure hope you're going down to the polls and voting for the right man today, young man?"

Suge followed suit and played the con as well. "Yes, sir. This is the first year I'm able to vote and I'm going to take full advantage of the opportunity. I think it's very important to have strong male role models in politics. It gives us hope and shows we are making strides as a Black Race."

"Good observation, son. You're a fine young man. I hope you won't be coming to run against me one day. I'd much rather have your contributions so we can work together instead of you as the competition. We need to work together as a community, not as greedy individuals. It's good to always have great friends in many places. Like you *Soog,* you showed me that you're my friend and I want to be a good friend to you. Now, I hear you may need my assistance. This is what I'm here to be: a true service to the community by complying with my supporters' needs, especially those that make such generous contributions to keep me in office as a man of the people and a man of my word. Now I want to help you but I have a very busy schedule today making appearances and shaking hands at the polls. By the way, where will you be voting today, son?"

Suge had to think quickly. He never registered to vote or planned to. It came to him from memory.

"I will be voting at my old school, Pasteur *Jr.* High," with a slight emphasis on Jr. High. "They've been voting there for years. And it's close to our home."

"Jr. High School? Hmm? Yeah, I'm familiar... You know it says here I have to talk to the voters in that neighborhood. Why don't you meet me at the polls at Pasteur Jr. High School? Do you still have any friends that attend the school? Uh, you know it's good to talk to the young potential voters out there early, and the old ones, too."

Suge didn't want to blow the chance to speak to Assembly Wright so he lied and said he still had friends there. All of our friends left there once we entered high school. Suge damn sure wasn't going to let any young girls get jacked off on at Pasteur on his watch so he hoped Mr. Wright wasn't trying to go there so he put the thought out of his mind. It was a long shot but if it worked, it was going to pay off big time.

As soon as Suge hung up, Christiane voiced her opinion. "I don't like that sick son of a bitch. I don't like the way his voice sounds. He's an evil bastard."

"Yeah, but he might can help. Now I wish I could have caught him in that compromising position," Suge wished out loud and was still upset with his rookie actions He still had a lot to learn about being a real player. A player was far more than a fancy title that comes with having more than one girlfriend.

"Definitely, baby. Dez would be free already."

"Are you riding down with us to the lawyer's office? 'Cuz depending on what time we finish up there, I'll probably have meet Assemblyman Wright soon after."

"I have to handle that business we discussed about the spa on Pico. The owner is being an asshole. He's thinking of not selling now. He can see the potential in it all of a sudden. He's looking for short-term investors but that's bullshit. He's trying to recruit better girls. I've seen his type before. Do you have time to run to the Fresh Poultry store on Western and Exposition?"

"Vons market is right down the street! It smells awful in that place. My father used to take me there and let me pick out the holiday turkey or chicken when I was little."

"They don't have what I need at Vons. This is uh, what you guys say it, Special. It's Special Order. I'm going to give you a note and you give it to Ramon. He knows what I need. Drop it back here before you go. Thank you, baby! You're so kind."

"You're pushing it baby, but I am not going to have fresh chicken in my hot trunk all day."

"Good. See you later, yeah?"

"Yeah Good luck with the spa, keep me posted."

$ $ $ $ $

Suge and I met at the lawyer's office. The rest of the crew had other business to tend to and it was better that way. It was no need to roll up there six deep.

"Damn, Suge you smell awful... like partridge! You just get finished fuckin'?"

"Trav, if I ever stumble across some pussy that smells like a fowl farm, trust me I won't be hittin' that. I am not Shannon. I had to run over to the old Fresh Poultry spot off Exposition, by the railroad tracks. Christiane needed some stuff from there. I just stood in there ten to fifteen waiting for the order and I smell like I have been working up in there on an 8-hour shift. You should smell the trunk of my car."

"Damn, you be fuckin' with all these foreign broads you better watch what you eat. Fuck around and catch the gout."

"Can't be no worse than this processed shit we live off of. At least these geese are fresh," Suge spoke the truth.

"Geese?"

The lawyer stepped in with a crooked look and untrustworthy aura that surrounded him like a cloud. He was much more relaxed in his speech after we put that retainer down. Lawyer Cohen briefed us on the case. Everything he told us was *on the record*. It didn't help us one bit. There weren't enough pieces to put together. The information just gave us an idea where Dez might have been at the time of the alleged murder. As of now Dez was still a prime suspect and from what we gathered it was something that happened a long time ago.

"Are you gentlemen familiar with a man by the name of Ronald Brown?"

Suge and I looked at each other and neither of us had a clue.

"He goes by the name of Noopy on the streets. He is a member of the Crip Gang and is supposedly affiliated with the South East Block Sect."

"That's a homeboy Dez fucks with on the Eastside," I informed Suge.

"Yeah I heard Dez speak his name, but I don't know that homie," Suge answered. I turned to Leo Cohen.

"We don't know him, but we heard of him. Why you ask?"

"Can we speak off the record now?" Leo Cohen leaned forward and looked us in our eyes as if he were checking to see if we had the beast in us. We nodded and he continued. "Ronald Brown got himself into a world of trouble. He was looking at 20 years easy. They offered him a one-way ticket to freedom and giving up Dez was the price he had to pay. Ronald claims he witnessed Dez commit multiple homicides and he knows all the locations where the guns are buried. Right now he's playing hardball with the detectives because he wants his case dropped completely. They are offering him ten years if he cooperates. This gives you a little time but not much to get rid of this problem. No guns, no witnesses, no case!"

$ $ $ $

We left Leo Cohen's office with mixed feelings. We knew we had to eliminate a problem but it didn't come with an easy solution. We weren't young locs anymore. This was some next level hit. We didn't have OGs to show us how to pull this off. We started Westside

Gangsters. We were living and learning. We couldn't just walk up to any old gangster and ask, *Hey, how do you kill a star witness locked in protective custody that snitched on your homeboy?*

We were already learning from Dez's situation we couldn't trust anybody outside of Westside with any information they can use against us. Muthafuckas nowadays are going for self. I didn't think I would see the day gangsters started snitching on each other so this was some new shit on the streets. The game was never played like that. It wasn't, but less than five months ago that Noopy's own homeboys would have killed him soon as they heard he was a rat. Dez put a lot of cheese in that rat's pocket too. They were living well on that impoverished part of town once Dez laced their hood with that good.

I took it upon myself to go to their hood on the Eastside and feel them out. Hopefully we can come to a peaceful agreement. Noopy had to get touched regardless. We wanted to give them enough respect to handle their snitch in-house. Suge was about to skip his meeting with Assemblyman Wright and roll to the Eastside with me. I encouraged him not to so at least we would feel comfortable knowing we examined all options before shit went from hectic to heinous. Soncho and Khan were the best soldiers to roll with. Shannon would create an enemy we didn't need. He would start the conversation rudely with his gun out. I already know how he gets down. But if shit gets thick, believe me, I will have my nigga nearby.

$ $ $ $

Suge arrived at our old alma mater Pasteur Jr. High behind schedule. Assemblyman Wright was out there shaking hands and kissing babies of the voters coming to the polls, as he seemed to be leaving. As Suge walked up, Wright shot him a sideways look but Suge didn't know what to make of it. This was a long shot anyway.

Shareece Wright was pretending not to pay Suge too much attention until one of the homies from PBG's little sisters that was volunteering that day ran up to Suge and spoke. That got Wright's attention. It was best that Assemblyman Wright knew how to pick his poison because he didn't play her like she was Sun. This girl's father and brother would have put that nigga's lights out forever right in front of the school in broad daylight just for knowing he was thinking about some shit like that.

"Hey *Soog*! Let me talk to you, son!" Shareece Wright waved him over as he was walking to his limousine.

"It's Su—never mind."

Shareece Wright wanted to take some pictures with a first time voter and Suge was his candidate. He put his arm around Suge and cheesed for the camera. He whispered in Suge's ear. "School lets out at 3 o'clock, right?"

"Yeah, why?"

Shareece Wright checked his watch. "I want to get out of here before all those bad kids come out of there and start jumping on my limo asking for a ride. Let's go have some lunch at Bob's Big Boy up the street on La Cienega on me. You look like you could use a good burger. You don't mind taking your car and following me, do you?"

$ $ $ $ $

"You have a collect call from an inmate in the Los Angeles County Jail. Will you accept?"

"Hey Shannon! Dez is calling collect from jail. Y'all ain't gonna keep putting all these expensive calls on my phone every time one of you knuckleheads get locked up. What the fuck they always got to call here for? I hope not for bail money. They will be dead in that bitch waiting for your cheap ass to bond them out." Pops complained even though that was one of the few bills he had now.

"Accept the call, Pops! You didn't say that shit when you got that DUI and I had to get you out of jail."

"I was calling my own house, muthafucka. I didn't call Dez or Soncho or his mama, I called my house. I paid for the collect call when I got home didn't I cuz it was on my bill in my muthafuckin house!"

"Ha ha ha! What up Pops? What you doing drinking Vodka and talking shit?" Dez asked once he put the call through and heard Pops talking crazy as usual.

"Ha-ha? Why you sound so happy? You're in jail, muthafucka, with no vodka to drink and nobody to talk shit to. You should be crying. So whatever the fuck I'm doing in my own house is better than what you're doing in the clink. What the fuck did you do anyway? Snatch some old lady's purse?"

"C'mon Pops, put Shannon on the phone. I don't have long."

"Oh yeah, I know that. You are going to cut this call real short. You can't pay for it with Zoom Zooms and Wham-Whams!" Pop's continued making the call more expensive as he talked. Dez only had one thing to say once he finally got on Shannon on the phone.

"Hey Shannon, we gots to get to that nigga by any means necessary—no matter the cost—or they are going to hit your boy with the kitchen sink."

"All day?"

"With no night!"

$ $ $ $ $

Suge and Assemblyman Wright ordered a couple of Bob's Big Boy Specials with salads and their famous bleu cheese dressing. We all discovered by accident at a Bob's Big Boy that french fries didn't always have to be eaten with ketchup. Steak cut fries dipped in the bleu cheese dressing was the bomb. It was creepy that Assemblyman

Wright demanded to be seated in the booth so he could watch all the young girls passing by and at the bus stop just leaving school.

"Boy, would you look at that young girl there? What are they putting in the milk for them to develop like that? You sure got it good in your day, son. I know you have a couple of young things sweet on you at that school. My daddy taught me that if it got hair mane, it's fair game." Shareece Wright joked, but it wasn't funny to Suge at all. Suge looked at sick tricks the same way Dez saw OGs that weren't wise: with disgust. Assemblyman Wright was trying to get Suge to get him some young snatch again without asking. He had no intention of listening to our Westside problems, but he owed Suge that much. But he also wanted to lend his ear as a down payment for another hookup. He gave Suge the courtesy to briefly explain Dez's situation. He thought we needed another permit. Soon as he heard *jail*, he excommunicated himself from that conversation all-together. He pretended to listen because he was in character. It was election time and helping the people was his job. The punk-ass Negro behind the façade was already preparing his exit speech with damn near a full plate of food left on the table.

"I'm sorry *Soog*-"

"It's Suge. You know, like Sugar. Suge." He corrected him twice because he no longer wanted to be nice.

"I'm sorry, *Suge,*" Shareece Wright said with sarcasm and continued. " I can't help you, I can't doing anything of that magnitude. You need to get your friend a good lawyer." But Suge knew he was lying because he had done it before.

A young girl that looked like she was Spanish and Black stopped at the bus stop. She was kind of homely looking not too stylish but she was cute, like a little sister cute. She wore studious-looking glasses. She must not have drunk the milk Shareece Wright referred to because she didn't have much of a developed body. She peeked in the window and saw Suge. She smiled and waved. Suge waved back. He didn't recognize her off hand but all the neighborhood kids start to look the same after a while. Shareece Wright paused to see if there was a connection between the two he could take advantage of. He laughed and said, "Now if you could get me next to that, I'll set your boy free as a bird." Even though he was joking, Suge did not like the way it sounded. He was still insinuating that there was a possibility to help us at the right price.

Suge got up to leave when Shareece got up to leave. Suge pleaded with him all the way out to the parking lot. Suge started talking money out of young desperation. He didn't know that was an under the table matter handled in a manner we hadn't seen yet. We had the tools to play in the game, but we were not in that league yet. But the word *money* did slow his walk out of Bob's Big Boy down a little bit.

They continued to talk in the parking lot. Suge felt the energy and knew he couldn't talk direct so he started subliminally throwing figures out there in a round about kind of way relating them to other things that got the fish sniffing at the bait.

That damn young girl at the bus stop started pacing back and forth with her Sony Walkman on as she waited for the bus. She glanced in their direction, smiled at Assemblyman Wright, and then quickly turned her head. Suge's words fell on deaf ears then.

Assemblyman Shareece Wright started feeling himself a little bit and his mind was racing with possibility. She couldn't possibly be choosing him over the young handsome heartthrob Suge. Shareece never had the ability to get a female other than his ugly wife to pay him any attention without a thousand dollars in his hand or from a favor. Shareece waited in anticipation hoping she turned around and looked their way again. After ten minutes, she turned back towards the bus stop and glanced again. She licked her lips slowly and shot another quick innocently seductive glance directly at Shareece Wright. He didn't need Suge's help this time. Suge immediately became a pest. The RTD bus pulled up and desperation flashed in Shareece's eyes.

He couldn't let that girl get away.

"Sir, can you help us?" Suge asked, sensing he lost him and he just had him so close to the hook. Suge never turned around to see the nice succulent bait that was luring his fish.

"Look, I told you I can't help you kid, I'm pressed for business!" Assemblymen Wright said as he scurried off to the bus stop.

"Oh? Okay!" Suge stated with wishful revenge. He felt more used than a politician's hoe.

The girl was just about to get on the bus and Assemblyman Wright put his hand gently on her shoulder and stepped on the bus in front of her. He encouraged every one to vote for him. He stepped off the bus and let the other passengers on as he shook hands and gave fake smiles. The young girl was the last passenger.

"Hi, today is your lucky day. Would you like to ride home in a limousine?"

"Wow! I'd get to ride that... *BIG* limousine over there?"

"And whatever else you want to do, you pretty thing. Let's go!"

$ $ $ $ $

Shannon was pissed that they didn't invite him to meet up with those southeast fools and come to an agreement. But with Shannon being Shannon, he decided he was going to trail us anyway and stay low key in the cut. He definitely had the discipline to do it but only when he wanted to do it. Shannon was looking to set some shit off that day. He was on one. He just bought a new Mack 11 too. A big kid with a new toy is no bueno. This meeting was not going to turn out right with Shannon in his mood.

Shannon strapped up and left his crib, but never made it off his block.

There was a White man sitting on the hood of his car, taking a drag off of a freshly lit cigarette. It'd been a couple of years and he had grown a goatee since Shannon had seen him last, but he remembered that muthafucka way before he spoke.

"How have you been, Shannon?" The man took another deep drag of his cigarette. "Do you remember me?"

$ $ $ $ $

We rolled over to the Eastside. Soncho and Dante felt we should have brought more homies just in case some shit jumped off. I had that feeling, too, but it wasn't burning in my gut. We were just going to talk and see where their heads were at. But my homies were right. We sometimes take a few of our new recruits and post them in different areas around the perimeter, but that's when we did business with a set that was deemed untrustworthy.

We even rode in Soncho's new Mercedes. We didn't want to spook those cats by rolling through in our low profile car. The white Benz was a symbol of peace. We just hoped they saw it that way. A lot of other niggas didn't think like us. We met up with them at Jessie Owens Park. It was 9-0's territory because neither of our sets had beef with them, so it was a good neutral location. It would be disrespectful to let off some shots and make their hood hot.

"Hey, what's up homie? I'm Trav, this is Dante, and that's Soncho."

"What up, cuz? What up cuz! What's Crippin'?" Seth accepted our greeting and returned the gesture with some weak half-ass handshakes. He was one of those young *I don't give a Fuck ass niggas* with a natural bad attitude even when he's happy. He looked tough. He had a mean face. We didn't know if it was from putting in work or if he was just the offspring of two rough looking mad face parents He wore a sweatshirt with khakis saggin', and a short Jeri Curl Natural that was glistening in the sun. He had some Brownie gloves on as more of a fashion statement than protecting his knuckles in a squab.

"I'm quite sure you know your Big Homie put his ass in a twist and in order for him to get straight again he had to put on that snitch jacket and give up our soldier Dez. Now I don't know the specifics of business y'all was doing with our homie, but I know for a fact business was good. Gangsters snitching on gangsters is not how the game is played. They must be executed with extreme prejudice. As a sign of respect, we come to you to ask if you are going to take care of this matter in house or leave him out there for the wolves to eat," I explained the situation.

"What the fuck you talking about, cuz? I don't understand all that military talk and shit. Ain't no snitches in my hood cuz! I don't know what you talkin' bout. All my homies are right here. What you getting' at cuz? Take care of what?"

"That's how you gon' play this homie? You gon' pretend like that nigga named Big Noopy ain't sittin' in protective custody right now singing to the Police?" Dante spoke up.

"Hey look cuz, I'm talking to homie over here in the pretty shirt!" Seth clowned and generated a lot of laughter. He looked back at me and said what was on his mind. "The Big Homie ain't snitched on nobody on this side of town. He ain't gave up no real Crips. Who gives a fuck about some Preppy dressed niggas on the Westside gang bangin' in Beverly Hills? That's some Buster shit for real. Are we supposed to take that serious? We laugh at little sets like yours. If we brought all the South East through there, we would crush that whole side of town like Hitler did the Jews," Seth concluded in his disrespectful manner

We see niggas like him all the time. We even have one like that on our set always talking shit 'cause he knows he has homies like us to hold him down. The way Seth started talking just let us know they were strapped up and had the upper hand. The situation got tense just that quick. I was ready to sock that little muthafucka in the mouth but I know his hands would pull out a pistol before he balled both fists to knuckle up.

"We didn't come here to create new enemies. We like to find ways to create new money. This is what we are in this game for, right? You know as well as I do you little greasy muthafuckas wasn't rolling like this until Dez laced you with that good shit. If that buster will snitch once its just a matter of time before he starts making deals to set y'all up," I stated, trying to use a little psychology on some young dangerous gangsters that only thought one way.

"Speaking of money, I hope y'all didn't come over here empty handed. We shouldn't even be talking this long. You ain't broke bread yet. You owe us something for your homie droppin' two of our homies. He even shot the homie that just touched down. Cuz didn't even get to smell fresh air. That's what this meeting is about, ain't it?"

He lost us with that one. We weren't about to pay that fool shit. We know what really happened. It was time to conclude this meeting before it got ugly.

But this little fool Seth kept running his mouth. "What you got? I think $50 G's and two of those chickens is reasonable. If not, we taking it to trial and we gon' get the restitution out you niggas. You are looking at the Star Witnesses right here. The homies and me was there when it all went down. So yeah fuck it, the Big Homie is PC'd up but your homie is on the Main Line in the Crip Module. You know we can touch him way faster than you can get to Big Noopy. We got numbers up in that bitch. We could have hit him already. Do y'all funny style niggas even have any gang affiliations? I ain't never seen no Cosby Kids Crips in the County Jail. Have y'all?" Seth clowned. He was full of jokes. Soncho was getting tired of his mouth to. I know he was thinking what I was thinking.

"You're a real comedian. We need to holler at some of your OGs 'cause you baby gangsters don't take this game serious enough," Soncho stated.

"Now the chubby nigga in the Potsie Sweater want to talk some gangster shit. You must be Fat Albert. What you want, nigga, some candy? I'll bring you a Twinkie when we come through to pick that up. Y'all got 24 hours to get that package together! This meeting is finished."

There was a silent standoff. We chose to speak with our eyes and scowl. They understood exactly what our facial expression was saying. They understood that if we gave them that package to save Dez, it was going to be considered a loan. We were going to be coming back for it eventually with interest. We kept our eyes locked on theirs giving them one last opportunity to see if they really wanted to take it where it didn't have to go. Three cars pulled in the parking lot with three to four passengers in each ride. We put our hands on our guns.

They were some older niggas. They all had at least ten years on us or they lived extremely hard lives. We assumed it was the OGs from their set. They didn't look like they came to welcome us to the Eastside but we knew from experience a conversation with an OG has a much better outcome than dealing with one of those little hardhead muthafuckas trying to earn some stripes.

They parked the cars and hopped out strapped. That's when we pulled our guns out. Seth and his young crew kind of tightened up, too, but we didn't even notice it. As they got closer, I didn't see anybody we knew personally but I did recognize a couple of faces I had seen around just from being in the game. One of those *friends of a friend* that you know that's not really a friend, just somebody you got introduced to. I knew of them like that. I knew for sure they weren't from Seth's hood. I've seen them around our way. These niggas was grown men.

The biggest and oldest looking ones walked over to Seth and had a little quiet talk with him. We kept our eyes on the rest of them. I don't know which one pulled the trigger but when Seth's blood splattered across my face, I thought a muthafucka spit on me and I got mad before I took cover. We had nowhere to run anyway. We had eleven guns of different kinds pointed at us at close range… both crews. The shooters walked over to us. They put guns to our foreheads. The one with the 9mm pressed up against my head looked at one of his henchmen and jerked his head to the right. We heard him say, "It's your lucky day. You little punks get the fuck outta here. Run!"

Two of the gunmen opened a small path in the circle and let Seth's homies go. They took off running at top speed. All that gangster shit and mad dogging they were doing to us was gone. They looked like scared little kids. We had no choice but to man up. We never dropped our weapons when they drew down on us. When the three old dudes walked up on us that was the best thing we had going. I had my Big Bad Boy pressed hard against the nuts of the nigga that had his pistol at my dome. Soncho had his 45 fitted perfect in some fool's belly button. Dante had his in homie's neck. If this was it, then so be it.

"These little niggas ain't no punks." The fool in my face stated to no one in particular.

"I told you. These little Young Westside Locs are raw. They might be a small crew but they do big things." A gunman co-signed our reputation.

"I don't give a fuck. They still little punks bringing that young shit to grown folks' business. Do y'all know who I am?"

"You look familiar but we don't know your names," I answered. But shit, we learned in this game early, it didn't even matter. Enemies that you didn't even know you have come gunning for you. This is the kind of shit that happens when you're Young Locs on the Westside.

Soncho was more pissed than scared with one gun pointed at the front of his head and another barrel pressed against the back of his head. Frustrated he just said, "Damn, I can't believe this shit just happened to us again!"

$ $ $ $ $

"Do you know who I am, sweetie?" Assemblyman Wright asked as he stripped down to his Fruit of the Loom white cotton briefs. The young girl was already naked and doing the lines of coke that Shareece Wright provided after she told him what kind of mood it puts her in.

"You're like the President of Los Angeles or something. I must confess. I've had a crush on you ever since you won that election thing. You looked so confident and powerful, and then my Mom, for crying out loud, noticed your bulge and said, *Whooo Assemblyman Wright likes to dress to his left.* I had no idea what she was talking about until she pointed. That was the first time I ever got wet. I never forgot that sensation. That's the moment I consider my first time."

The young girl was seductive and intoxicated. Shareece Wright was past confident. They were at an undisclosed location near Chinatown where a lot of powerful men pay a lot of money to keep their sick personal vices private.

"Well, it looks like your fantasy is about to come true," Shareece stated as he pulled down his briefs. That middle school girl's young body gave him a powerful erection. He was scared he might cum too quick. He snorted two lines to give him a little boost of energy and cloud his vision. He was still a 55-year-old man in the bed with a girl younger than all three of his daughters. Shareece Wright dipped his index finger in the powder, but instead of rubbing it on his gums like most folks do, he rubbed it around the head of his dick just in case. He took all precautions to prevent an embarrassing moment like cumming in under two minutes.

"Damn, Mommy was right. I hope I can take all that in."

Shareece Wright's ego was now out of control. Nobody had ever complimented the size of his manhood before. He climbed on top of the young girl thinking *I'm about to fuck the shit out of this young pussy.* He entered the girl fairly easy. She wasn't as tight or he wasn't as big as he thought. Shareece wasn't in the best shape and didn't have enough arm strength to ride it like a warrior. He laid flat on top of her sweating profusely, grunting, and breathing hard. He had that fast, short-stroke fucking style.

For a young girl, she was extremely wet. After a minute, Shareece Wright realized that fucking the shit out of that young girl sounded good when he thought it but never knew it would happen literally. And now the young girl's pussy started giving out the foulest odor he had ever smelled in his life. It didn't smell like period juice. It kept getting stronger and stronger. He had to decide if that young pussy was worth it. Even in his sick condition, he knew something had to be wrong with it. It was starting to smell like a damn petting zoo in the room. He wanted to get that nut off, but after another minute the odor just got too pungent.

"Gotdamn bitch! Did you wash your pussy?" He stated angrily as he rolled over off of her.

The young girl was on the bed in a pool of blood having tremors and shaking but it wasn't because the sex was great. She was trying to swallow her tongue. She was having an epileptic seizure. Shareece Wright's wife had them so he realized what was happening. He actually had a spoon he kept in the inside pocket of his suit jacket just for that reason, but the amount of blood on the bed and all over his lower torso was sickening. Shareece Wright checked her ID. There was a sticker on it that stated she suffered from seizures.

But Shareece never went into panic mode because even if she had died, the place where he was at took care of little things like that. Bitches OD'd off drugs and old men die all the time after being strangled and tortured by prostitutes with whips and leather spikes. Shareece Wright took a shower, got dressed, and dropped $100 on the table never even looking in her direction. The bloody, foul-smelling scene was still pictured in his mind. He was disgusted. He told her to go wash her stinkin' ass and a driver would take her back to the bus stop. He left that foul-smelling room in an angry mood.

He drove himself home to his wife, feeling guilty as he always did. He nursed his pain from guilt with scotch and water and then he went to La Louisiana in Windsor Hills a few blocks from his home in

Baldwin Hills. He pulled up in the parking lot and got out of the car. He felt a blow to the back of his head from a blunt object but it didn't knock him out. His mouth and eyes was duct taped, and he was in the back of a trunk before he knew what hit him.

$ $ $ $ $

It seemed like days, but only six hours passed before the abductors snatched the fresh duct tape off of his eyes hard as they could. Some hairs from his eyebrows and eyelashes were plucked with it. That shit hurt like a muthafucka. The abductors were wearing ski masks. It took Assemblyman Wright a minute to get his vision back and he had a headache that was this big. He was in what looked to be a warehouse or storage facility of some sort. There was a TV in the room and the two, maybe three, abductors.

Shareece Wright was connected. Even if he died that day those abductors would be caught and eventually executed.

"You guys are way out of your league. Do you know who I am?"

One of the abductors turned on the television to Channel 2. There was a Sig Alert about a young girl that was kidnapped after school. He turned to Channel 4, and it was the same thing but in more detail. He turned to Channels 5, 11, 9, and 13 and it was the same thing.

"I know who you are. You are the sick bastard that molested my little sister and damaged her insides, you sick fuck. She'll never be able to have kids in life if she makes it. She's in intensive care fighting for her life. If she dies, your whole familia will suffer for months while we make you watch from your jail cell. It will not be a quick death. You are going to jail, you sick bastard."

Assemblyman Wright was only a little nervous now. Not because of what he did to the little girl; these abductors did not sound black. They sounded like they were El Salvadorian or Cuban and they are hard to find. They could flee the country at anytime. Regardless, they could never prove it. They would never be able to prove that the private club existed. Undisclosed location means just that. They had no evidence or witnesses. Shareece knew they were looking for a payday. Some poor muthafuckas from El Salvador or where the hell they were from will forget all about that shit for about five grand. That wasn't shit. He knew what time it was.

"All right, all right! So how much do you guys want to make this misunderstanding go away?"

The abductor tuned the television to channel 3. There was a snowy picture on the screen. He popped a videotape in the VCR. The picture was scrambled for a moment, then it became very clear.

Assemblyman Wright was not prepared for what he was about to see.

"OH GOD!"

THIS STORY WILL BE CONTINUED...

Soncho

Shannon

JACKER
MAD

KHAN

Dante

Dez

SUGE

DANGEL
BEATS

KRISTIAN
BINNS

TRAV & TONI

WEST LOS SCANDELOUS PART III
The TRILOGY

Coming Soon

Special Shout out to JELANI, KAHMONE, DONNIE BILLS, BLUE HEFFNER, LAIR ONLY, ITS KID LA, SONCHO, BIG BO DANGEL BEATS, PAPA JUGGY, KRISTIAN BINNS, NIKKO DE, RORY MACK, PIMP DUBIE, BOO KAPONE, GINA & DAYNA, AC the PD, SMOOTH MELLOW, the God RAHEEM, and UNIVERSAL for taking this Book to the Big Screen and appreciating the blessing that was graced upon us. DELICIOUS PIZZA, MIKE & RICK ROSS: THE LOVE IS ALWAYS THERE. MID CITY PICO DELI, PIPS on LaBrea, SADOU'S HAIR ARTISTRY FOR HELPING US WHEN WE NEEDED YOU THE MOST, DANIEL KIM for putting the exclamation point on it!!, ALL MY BROSHOTS AT QSR SYSTEMS, the Supreme Blessing that put the series in MOTION, and to all the locations WE GANGSTERED TO MAKE THIS SERIES A SUCCESS...

hey, we had to do what we had to do to make it do what it do!

WEST LOS SCANDELOUS The Series
aka YOUNG LOCS ON THE WESTSIDE PART II

SHANNON .... DONNIE BILLS @mrwestmade

TRAV ....JELANI @jaybazz_

TONI ....KAHMONE @kahmone_calibaby

DEZ ....MARK @BLUEHEFFNER

LAIR ....LAIR @lair_only

KHAN .... RICH @ITS KID RICH

SONCHO .... SONCHO @bigbird_soncho

ALSO AVAILABLE

Legendary grew up throughout the Los Angeles area leaving his mark from Inglewood to West LA. Raised by a single mother, he grew up as an only child but not a lonely child. Even though he came from the stereotypical ghetto neighborhood with gangs, drugs, poverty, and prostitution, his surroundings had no influence on his writing style at all.

"I lived in the hood. Everybody knew me; I was an active participant in hood activities but it was never an event that made me say 'Hey, I want to write stories about these conditions one day!' That ain't shit and too many lames do it. I write about people I meet that just happen to live in those areas. I won't describe the background scenes in my books too often but the characters themselves are very detailed."

Legendary discovered his knack for wordplay when his 5th grade teacher intercepted a love letter he wrote to his sweetie. She sent the letter home to his mom. Legendary didn't get in trouble for writing a seductive love letter at 10 years old. The teacher and his mom were upset with him because they never had a man write them a letter worded so beautifully. Usually that's when the adult steps up and notices the talent. Needless to say, due to a bitter teacher that was lonely, Legendary was never encouraged to continue his writing even though he had a special gift.

Eleven years later, Legendary was on tour, dancing with his group, the world famous Soul Brothers when Rapper Def Jef encouraged him to write full novels. Legend took that seriously. He immediately wrote two short gangster novels and was labeled by his peers as the 2nd coming of D. Goines and Iceberg Slim and he didn't even know who they were at the time!

Legendary continued to hone in on his craft over the years and is the author of several published novels.

Today, Legendary still lives and works in Los Angeles where he serves as the Director of Operations for Go Beyond the G.A.M.E. Student Athlete Mentoring Program. He received his BA at Cal State University Dominguez Hills in Carson, and also works in post production in the TV industry. Legendary is immensely proud of his son Jelani, whom he raised as a single dad. Legendary loves to root for his favorite football team the Baltimore Ravens, and continues to tour the world dancing with the Soul Brothers on the Golden Era of Hip Hop circuit.

www.ingramcontent.com/pod-product-compliance
Lightning Source LLC
Chambersburg PA
CBHW031546040426
42452CB00006B/201